RECOLLECTIONS OF
AN IRISH DOCTOR

Photo. Elliott & Fry.

Lombe Atthill
M.D

Some time President of the Royal College of Physicians Dublin,
President of the Royal Academy of Medicine Ireland,
and Master of the Rotunda Hospital.

RECOLLECTIONS OF AN IRISH DOCTOR

LOMBE ATTHILL, M.D.

With an foreword by
HUGH W.L. WEIR

BALLINAKELLA PRESS
WHITEGATE, CO. CLARE

Recollections of an Irish Doctor
Additional material © 2007, Hugh Weir
Whitegate
Co. Clare
Ireland

ISBN 0 946538 48 4

Limited edition of 750 copies

Origination by SUSAN WAINE
Typeset in Adobe Garamond and Augustea
Reprinted by ßETAPRINT
Bluebell Industrial Estate, Dublin 12, Ireland

PREFACE

The author of these reminiscences, Dr. Lombe Atthill, a distinguished ornament of the medical profession in Ireland, was born in 1827 and died, suddenly, in 1910. He placed the manuscript of this book in the publishers' hands shortly before his death, and the arrangements for its issue were completed by his widow.

A FOREWORD

$\mathcal{S}$ince the republication of such popular biographical works as *An Irish RM* and the many diaries recording the experiences of different types of people, I felt a desire to re-offer *Recollections of an Irish Doctor* to readers of such works. A rare book published in 1911, it vividly describes the daily life, diet and material culture of the pre-famine period in the north-west corner of Co. Fermanagh where the author's father was a Church of Ireland rector.

Lombe Atthill's parents were The Reverend William born in 1774 to Anthony John Atthill of Brandiston Hall, Norfolk, and Henrietta Margaret Eyre (*nee* Maunsell) whose father was rector of Drumcree, Portadown. Lombe, born in 1827, was the sixth of their seven boys. Brought up in Magheraculmoney Rectory, and educated in England, at Enniskillen, and at the Royal College of Physicians in Dublin, in 1844 he was apprenticed to Dublin Surgeon Maurice Collis. Three years later he married Jane, daughter of Fermanagh Crown Solicitor Lowther Brien and of his wife Margaret (*née* Harper). Two of James' uncles, Edward Henry Brien and Robert Brien, were naval surgeons while other family members either served in the Forces or the Church.

The first part of *Recollections* is a fascinating record of life and times in the early nineteenth century as seen through young, if privileged eyes. The book continues with descriptions of the poverty in urban Dublin, the famine and early experiences as a General Practitioner in Co. Offaly as well as the capital's professional and social life. Dr. Atthill continued a distinguished career as a gynaecologist and was to become Master of Dublin's Rotunda Hospital and President of both the Royal College of Physicians and President of the Royal Academy of Medicine.

Posthumously published in 1911, Lombe Atthill's *Recollections of an Irish Doctor* is a valuable, if little known, source for Irish social history.

HUGH W.L. WEIR

Editor and Publisher
Ballinakella Press

CONTENTS

RECOLLECTIONS OF AN IRISH DOCTOR

Contents

RECOLLECTIONS OF AN IRISH DOCTOR

INTRODUCTION

I can quite understand someone taking up this book and, after reading a page here and there, laying it down and saying, "How could anyone take the trouble of writing out this? there is nothing new or novel in it, and the writer does not seem even to have been acquainted with the leading people of his day." All quite true; it merely narrates incidents in the ordinary life of an ordinary man. Nor is it easy to say why it was written; probably the chief factor being, that at the end of a long and busy life, when old age and failing powers compel the adoption of one of inactivity, the mind, no longer occupied with the interests and anxieties incidental to the practice of a profession, reverts to the past. Then the memories of things long past and forgotten recur, or perchance are recalled by some little incident, in a quite unexpected manner and with wonderful vividness. To record these became a recreation to me.

Then I had often thought, during the later years of my professional life, that an outline of the difficulties and disappointments which so discouraged me at its commencement, if published, might perhaps encourage some of those similarly circumstanced—some who. relying on themselves, fail to realise that One higher than they directs their ways—and thus I might help them to look to Him for guidance.

I accordingly wrote some articles which appeared in the *British Medical Journal* a year ago (1909). These articles elicited kind letters from various medical friends, and I had some copies reprinted for private circulation. But this caused a difficulty, for as they contained much purely professional matter, not suited for the general reader, I had to refuse to give copies to various friends and relatives who wished for them.

During the last year or two I had in a desultory way, written my recollections of what I had heard in my childhood of my father's career. Of himself he ever spoke but little; but his graphic descriptions of the state of Ireland when he first came to it, had made a deep impression on my mind, and my children and friends having from time to time expressed their wishes that I would publish these, with memories of my own early years, I do so now, with no little hesitation, adding something of which had already appeared in the pages of the journal alluded to above.

The Victorian era, over the whole of which my memory extends, has been the most marvellous period in the world's history. In the brief space of sixty years, as a consequence of the many great discoveries and astonishing advances made in all departments of science, everything has changed.

My earliest recollections are connected with the talk about the recent opening of the Manchester and Liverpool Railway, and I remember well my being given a cotton handkerchief, on which that event was depicted, printed at the time in Manchester. So I have been cognisant of the development of railway travel from its earliest period, when twenty miles an hour was a wonder.

I remember the starting of the first steamship that crossed the Atlantic and the anxiety for news of her safety. I remember going through the dockyard at Chatham and seeing, I suppose, half a dozen ships of war in the process of being built, and the "London," a 90-gun man-of-war, launched only the day before. No one dreamed that ere a quarter of a century would have elapsed "the Wooden Walls of England" would be things of the past.

Then after a long interval came the astounding announcement that, by the aid of electricity, words and messages could be transmitted with incredible rapidity: and the electric telegraph was established, its value doubted by many, its use objected to by some. My brother went to America in 1837. The voyage, a favourable one, occupied five weeks, and the news of his arrival took many more days to reach us than it would take minutes to transmit it now.

Truly he must be destitute of all power of observation

who is unable to realise the truth of that prophetic utterance, that in the last days "many shall run to and fro, and knowledge shall be increased."

LOMBE ATTHILL, 1910

RECOLLECTIONS OF AN IRISH DOCTOR

CHAPTER I

IRELAND A HUNDRED YEARS AGO

Born in George IV.'s reign—My fifth birthday—Sir Robert Peel-Recollections of my father—Accession of Queen Victoria—Rev. Charles Simeon—My father takes holy orders and is made chaplain to an Irish bishop—The Irish Channel passage occupies two weeks—Ignorance of the poor Irish—Hedge schoolmasters—Deplorable state of the Church—Church livings as political rewards—The peace of decay and death in the Church—The bullet-marked parsonage—My father a second Oberlin—Building the first day school—Movement for promoting Sunday schools—My childhood's recollections and my father's death—The potato famine.

I WAS BORN in 1827, George the Fourth being still on the throne. Now my memory, while defective as to recent events, is unimpaired as to many which occurred over seventy years ago; thus I remember distinctly being carried round the room, seated in my little armchair, by my elder brothers, on the fifth anniversary of my birthday, that important event having been forgotten till dinner was over. I was the youngest of ten surviving children, and my eldest brother was twenty years my senior.

Even more clearly do I remember the advent to power for the first time of Sir Robert Peel— in 1834—this being impressed on my childish memory in consequence of the laughter excited by my asking an elder brother who had taken me on his knee during breakfast time, on the morning of his arrival from Dublin by the night mail, if he had heard "that Sir Robert P. had come in." I had heard so much about Sir Robert having "come in" that I thought I should communicate the news to him, though what "coming in" meant I knew not. Great was my shame at being so laughed at, but then I was barely seven years old. Truly a child's sense of ridicule must be acute, that such an incident should be so clearly remembered after the lapse of so many years!

Next, I have a vivid recollection of the annular eclipse of the sun which I now know occurred on May 15, 1834; and of the excitement caused in the parish by my father announcing on the previous Sunday that it would take place on that day week. and that, in order that the con-gregation should not be disturbed, Divine service would on that day commence at eleven instead of twelve o'clock, which, for the convenience of members of the congre-gation living at a distance, was the usual hour.

Many disbelieved him. Of course it proved to be true.

If was a bright sunny day; the eclipse commenced at about 3 o'clock, and we children watched with great anxiety for the event, armed with pieces of smoked glass which had been prepared beforehand. It seems to me but as yesterday that I stood beside my father as he explained to me, as it grew dark, how the moon was coming in front of the sun. Then we saw the sun looking like a mere crescent, and finally the ring of light appeared all round the dark body which he told us was the moon.Equally well do I remember hearing of the accession of Queen Victoria to the throne. My father and mother, having to pay a visit, took me in the carriage with them. We stopped in the village while my father went into the post office for letters, and coming out with the newspaper in his hand, read out the announcement that King William was dead and that the Princess Victoria had been proclaimed Queen. The news was nearly a week old, so slowly did it travel in those days.

My father was the last of the elder branch of an old Norfolk family, which had been settled in that county for centuries. Born in 1774, he was left fatherless when but four years old, with a sister a year or two older. This sister lived, unmarried, to be ninety-six years old. My grandmother marrying again very soon, and the match being disapproved of by my father's family, the children were taken charge of by their uncle, a leading surgeon in Norwich, and brought up with his family.

What his uncle's ideas of education were I know not, but at any rate he sent him at an early age to school at Kirkheaton, near Huddersfield, in Yorkshire, where he remained till he was sixteen and a half years old.

He seems to have been kindly treated while at school and happy enough, but certainly was taught very little, for he told me himself that his classical acquirements when he went up to Cambridge straight from school were very poor, while of mathematics he knew absolutely nothing, of Euclid, not even the first proposition; and he felt his ignorance greatly on his first arrival at the university.

Fortunately he had a friend there, a Norfolk man, who, like himself, had gone to Caius and Gonville Colleges, and who had been there for a couple of terms. This man took compassion on my father and offered to read with him for a while. But this relation of pupil and teacher was of but brief duration, though their friendship lasted till the death of the latter, for my father having mastered the six books of Euclid in a week, his friend said he thought the pupil could now get on without him. So he did, and to some purpose, for he gained a scholarship the following year. And at the degree examination in 1795 when his friend, Mr. Woodhouse, was senior wrangler and first Smith's Prizeman, my father came out second wrangler and second Smith's Prizeman.

It is rather a coincidence that not only were they both

Norfolk men, and both members of the same College; both were also born in the same month, though Mr. Woodhouse was the senior by a year (born April 28, 1773, my father on April 17, 1774). Both, too, were elected Fellows of their College. My father was elected in 1797, Mr. Woodhouse not till the following year, 1798. I know not why he was elected in preference to his senior, whom my father always spoke of in high terms.

At this date Charles Simeon was rector of Trinity Church, Cambridge, and was labouring with the greatest earnestness and zeal to rouse the Church of England from the dreadful state of apathy into which it had fallen. My father, coming under his influence, became deeply imbued with the truths of the gospel of Jesus Christ, and he determined to devote his talents to spreading the gospel, and his life to labouring in his Master's cause. Accordingly he took holy orders. Very soon a fitting opening was made for him in Ireland, for Dr. Porter, a relative, having been promoted to the bishopric of Clogher, he invited my father to go with him as his chaplain. This offer was accepted, and he followed the bishop to Ireland. This was in 1798.

The journey to any part of Ireland was in those days a serious matter. First, a tedious cross-country route to Holyhead had to be accomplished on heavy lumbering coaches, the journey from Cambridge occupying three days at the least. The Menai Bridge was not built till long after, and as the ferry boat could not always cross the straits, a delay of hours might occur there. Then the packets to Dublin were small, and dull sailers; and unless with a fair wind, the voyage to Howth or to the Pigeon House, which were the points the captains of these small vessels aimed at reaching, was often prolonged to days.

On either the second or third occasion of his crossing the channel my father, on reaching Holyhead, found such a gale blowing from the west that he was forced to remain at the little hotel there until it abated. One morning he was roused at daybreak and told that the packet which had been detained by the storm, would sail in half an hour. He hurried on board, and, with a strong but fair wind, had a rapid passage and arrived at the Pigeon House Fort, at the entrance of the Liffey, just one hour after the packet which had sailed five days before them arrived. Charles Dickens, in one of his works, gives a vivid description of the miseries endured by passengers during these voyages to Ireland.

Then, too, there was always the possibility of provisions running short. Nothing in the shape of food was provided for passengers. Each brought his or her own store, and sometimes these slender stores became exhausted; then ship's biscuits would form the only procurable food.

So late as in the year 1814 this mishap befell an Army surgeon, who, in his old age, narrated to me the troubles he endured in a voyage from Bristol to Cork on his return after serving through the Peninsular War. He had calculated that they might possibly occupy as much as five or six days at sea, and provided food accordingly, as also fodder for a fine mule he was bringing from Spain. But the fates were adverse, for a fortnight elapsed ere they readied their destination; all provisions, even the stores carried by the packet, were exhausted, and the poor mule was all but starved; but I believe he was landed alive.

An old gentleman whom I knew very well in my youth told me that before the introduction of steam, lie remembered, on one occasion, twenty-one days to elapse without the arrival of a mail in Dublin from England; he had read the statement allowing this to be so on a board fixed outside the general post office, on which used to be recorded daily the dates and hours at which packets arrived and departed and the number of niails due.

The diocese of Clogher, which roughly speaking comprised the counties of Fermanagh, Tyrone, and Monaghan, contained a large Protestant population, sunk, however, in the grossest ignorance. If at the end of the eighteenth century the Church of England was destitute of religious life, the Irish branch of it was sunk to the lowest depths of spiritual degradation, mainly due to the absolute indifference of the great majority of both clergy and laity to religion. The peasantry were ignorant to a degree hardly possible to be conceived of in the present day.

It was only in the larger towns that any means of educating the poor existed, other than that afforded by the "Hedge schoolmasters," a class of men themselves little above actual beggary, who wandered about the country, imparting their own scanty knowledge to the children of those who would supply-them with food and afford them a lodging. One of the last of this class came under my care so late as 1850. Now they are extinct. No wonder that a hundred years ago few could read and fewer write!

But if the peasantry were ignorant, the state of the Church was still more deplorable. The bishops were nearly all Englishmen, selected not for their fitness, but because they were related to some politicians who demanded from the minister of the day a bishopric for a son, a brother or other relative, in return for his vote and influence in Parliament. Most of these bishops disliked Ireland, in which they had to reside, far from the attractions of London, and few of them cared about the spiritual welfare of their dioceses, and for the most part exercised their patronage from personal or political motives.

Whether it was my father's brilliant career at Cambridge or his well-known piety which influenced the bishop who made choice of him as his chaplain I am unable to say, but certain it is that my father's arrival happened at a critical period in the history of the Church, and that he materially assisted in the movement, then commencing, to infuse life and a truly spiritual religion into the Irish Church.

It is true, no doubt, that at this time there were no disputes in the Church—all was peace; but it was peace the result of lethargy so profound as to simulate death. Bishop Ingram aptly describes such peace. He says: "There have been in the Church times of peace, which were not times of true peace, when the world and the Church made friends—when there were no ritual disputes or aggrieved parishioners, but only because no one cared what happened; when the standard of worship had been lowered to meet the slackness of the day." It was this false peace my father and a few Christian men, clergymen and laity, set about disturbing.

My father often spoke to me in his declining years of the sad state of Ireland at the date of his entering on the duties of chaplain to the bishop on him devolved the duty of examining the candidates for ordination, and he learned with amazement that this had been considered a mere form. When he determined not to treat it as such, and rejected several candidates, there arose something like a mutiny in the diocese. The bishop, however, supported him, and though it entailed on my father for a time a vast amount of annoyance he gained the day, and so far as his own diocese was concerned a better class of men presented themselves for ordination. One of the rejected candidates wrote him a most insulting letter, to which he did not reply. After a lapse of more than twenty years he received another letter from the same man, in which the latter expressed his gratitude to my father for having rejected him, saying that his having done so first led him to think that there was something more in ordination that the mere qualifying for preferment in the Church and that these thoughts in time led to his becoming a Christian, in the true acceptation of that term.

After filling for six years his trying post as chaplain, the bishop presented him with a living. The glebe house was small and inconvenient, and in a somewhat isolated situation, without shed or tree near it. On visiting it he found it in bad repair, the ceilings of several rooms showing the marks where they had been struck by bullets, while the hall door had been badly battered. In fact the house looked more like a dilapidated police barrack than a parsonage.

The explanation was simple. Although the actual rebellion of 1798 had been crushed after a brief campaign, it had been carried on in a desultory way for a considerable time subsequently; and the previous rector, a Mr. Johnston, fearing an attack from one of the numerous bands of rebels who for a considerable time roamed about the country, placed his house in a state capable of being defended, not that he was unpopular, but because these bands were in the habit of attacking any house from which they thought arms could be obtained.

Mr. Johnston's precautions were justified; his house was surrounded one night, and the demand that all his arms be handed out being refused, the house was fired on. This was replied to by Mr. Johnston and his gardener, the former from the upper, the latter from the lower story, Mrs. Johnston loading the now obsolete flint guns they had for her husband, a boy loading for the gardener. This desultory firing was continued on both sides for more than an hour; then the rebels, seeing that they could not thus succeed, made a rush, and attempted to sledge in the hall door; but Mr. Johnston had foreseen and provided for such an attempt, and had made a small opening just over the door, through which he now thrust the muzzle of one of the old-fashioned blunder busses, loaded with balls and slugs, and fired. The discharge took effect, for blood and brain were found adhering to the door next morning.

The rebels after this went off, carrying their dead or wounded with them; and not long after, a party of military made their tardy appearance, the firing having been heard in the village a mile off in which they were quartered. The officer explained that the delay in relieving them was due to the fact that the troops had been harassed by being drawn out night after night by the firing of guns only to find it to be a mere ruse, and that now they did not turn out till satisfied that a real attack was being made. Although this attack had occurred two or three years before Mr. Johnston's death, no attempt to repair the damage done had been made.

It was to this half barrack, half parsonage and much-dilapidated house that my father brought his young wife, to whom he had been married in the year 1805, and settled down to the life of a country clergyman, amongst a population ignorant to an extreme degree, steeped in poverty, and in truth only half civilised and liable at any moment to be excited to acts of violence. He, however, never once was insulted, threatened or obstructed in any way. This, no doubt, was mainly due to the fact that, though a perfect stranger, he came with the character of being a sincere Christian, one anxious for both the temporal and spiritual welfare of his parishioners and ready to help them to the utmost of his power.

Fifteen years later he moved to another parish, attached to which was a larger and more commodious glebe house. Here he at once set about to try and improve the wretched farming as practised by his ignorant parishioners, while he earnestly laboured for their spiritual welfare. My father always reminded me of what I have since read of Oberlin. Like him, while earnest in his main work, that of a minister of Christ, he laboured to elevate the degraded and neglected population amongst whom he was placed. He planted trees on the glebe lands and around the house, and succeeded in getting not a few of his parishioners to follow his example. He also took much trouble to get improved methods of farming adopted, for cultivation when he first came was of the most primitive kind. He had, moreover, a slight knowledge of medicine, picked up while he was a Fellow of Caius College; and as there was no doctor within miles, he soon gained both the confidence and gratitude of the poor, whom he doctored to the best of his ability. Indeed such a reputation did he gain that when a good many years later a dispensary was opened in the village, and a qualified medical man resided in the district, he experienced the greatest difficulty in inducing the poor to avail themselves of his services. It was probably from my father I inherited my taste for the medical profession, for even as a little boy I used to help him to make up medicines for the poor.

But it was to the work of the ministry that he devoted his best energies. The years spent as chaplain to the bishop had not been idle ones, for he had devoted his spare hours to study, nearly wholly to that of the Bible. At that time, too, he taught himself Hebrew, and was thus enabled to read the Scriptures in the original tongue. He had gained also the reputation of being, what he really was, an eloquent speaker and preacher, and was invited to preach in Dublin and elsewhere. Dr. Carson, for many years Vice-Provost of Trinity College, Dublin, gave me a newspaper, printed before I was born, announcing that a charity sermon would be preached in St. George's Church, Dublin, "by the Rev. W. Atthill," on the following

Sunday; and my friend, the Rev. Ralph Harden, a copy of the report of the meeting held in 1814 in Dublin "To promote the establishment of the Hibernian Church Missionary Society," in which appears the speech my father made in support of the first resolution; while in a letter written to me by my old friend, Dr. Stack, ex-bishop of Clogher, the following passage occurs: "I once asked the Primate (Beresford) who was the best preacher he ever heard; after thinking a minute he replied, 'Well, I have heard so-and-so, and can hardly say'; then he immediately added, 'Yes, I can tell you: William Atthill.'" This, of course, was said many years after my father's death.

But he was a most retiring "man, and it was only when he considered it a duty that he could be induced to leave home; seldom, indeed, failing till his health broke down to preach twice each Sunday in his own church, and also during the week in one other of the villages situated at a distance from his church; sometimes in a school-house or, failing that, in a room. He never wrote a sermon or brought notes into the pulpit, but devoted some hours regularly every forenoon to study, preparing the subjects on which he intended next to preach.

As to his parochial work, that he did most methodically. The Church services had been conducted in the most slovenly and irregular manner, and as very few of the congregation could read, the responses were made by the old clerk, who, there being no possibility of having any kind of music, also "raised" the psalm tunes to the best of his ability. The services, though no doubt dull, were very reverently conducted, and the congregation, which soon became a large one, very attentive. Holy Communion was regularly celebrated on the first Sunday in each month; previously it had only been at festivals— indeed, I think, only at Christmas and Easter. Baptism, which had been sadly neglected, soon became general. As to confirmations—well, the less said of them, the better. This I know, that for years before my father's death no confirmation had been held in his parish, the then bishop always making excuses when pressed to come. I was not confirmed till I was twenty, and then in England by the Archbishop of York. On one occasion the children gathered from three large parishes, and, I among them, assembled for confirmation, when, after waiting for hours, a servant in livery rode up to say that his lordship, not feeling well, had stopped at Enniskillen, fourteen miles off, and was not coming on. I have reason to believe he was not really ill, but he was always fancying himself ill, especially when called on to take a little trouble; he was a "lord" as well as a bishop.

There was no school in the whole of my father's large parish when he first came there, but he succeeded ere long in getting one built; and though there was great difficulty in obtaining a master, teaching proceeded regularly, so far as reading, writing, and some arithmetic were concerned. Then about the year 1810 the movement to promote the establishment of Sunday schools commenced, and in this movement he took an actual part; they proved a great success. Before his death three secular and three Sunday schools were established in his parish.

My father knew personally every family in his huge parish, which, though narrow, was fourteen miles long. There was but the one church in it, situated nearly in the centre; but he succeeded in having church built at each extremity, a district in each case being detached from his parish, and a similar portion from the adjoining ones, thus virtually creating two new parishes.

He died at the age of seventy-two, of a very painful disease, due, I believe, to fatigue and exposure during his long daily rides, taken in all weathers, visiting his flock: not the sick alone, but also those in health. A more humble and sincere Christian than he never lived, nor one more devoted to his Master's service.

As a little child I well remember his often taking me up as he sat on a chair with one leg crossed over the other, and seating me on his foot as it was raised by the other leg from the floor. Then he would give me a ride, holding me on with both hands, and saying all the time,—

"There go the mail coaches up and down every day, and they have four horses, and they have long tails; and the guard sits behind, and he has a red coat, and he blows the horn; and the coachman whips the horses, and the horses go a-gallop, a-gallop, a-gallop."

I can picture him standing up so straight, with his clean-shaved face and high forehead, looking down on his little son, and then, bending down, would clasp my two hands in his and turn me a somersault between his legs. This feat used to delight me even more than the rides on his foot. I only remember my father as an old man. He was tall and spare, but muscular, and to the very last his carriage was as straight and upright as that of any youth. He was bald, and had become so when only thirty. My feelings towards him as a "child were of great affection and great reverence—of affection in consequence of his invariable gentleness with us children. I never remember him punishing me. Once only he raised his hand to me. I must have been sixteen, and spoke disrespectfully in his presence to my mother. Being close to me he struck my cheek with a smart blow of his open hand, and spoke a few stern words. Then he left the room. I soon went out of it, too, when he called me into his study, to say that he regretted his hasty act as being unbecoming a Christian; then, having said a few kindly words pointing out my fault, he dismissed me, with my affection and reverence for him increased.

His death was a great blow, for I loved him, and my grief was great and sincere; and it is still my happiest memory to call to mind his laying his hands on my head a few months before his death, blessing me and saying, I was the greatest comfort he had in his life. He had been greatly pleased at the reports he received of my steady industry, and at my having gained the hospital prize in clinical surgery awarded at the end of the previous session.

But I believe that God in His mercy called him at this juncture from the scene of his earthly labours, and saved him from witnessing the calamities coming on Ireland. He died (February, 1847) just as the awful effects of the blight of the potato crop in the previous autumn were declaring themselves, to be followed by the even more terrible epidemic of fever, which swept away hundreds of thousands of its poverty-stricken inhabitants; while many thousands more fled its shores, seeking a new home in America, too often to encounter hardships, want, and even death, in New York and other seaports, into which these helpless emigrants crowded, and beyond which want of means prevented their going.

CHAPTER II

CHAPTER II

COUNTRY LIFE IN IRELAND UNDER GEORGE III AND IV

Primitive ploughs—Old Irish carts—Improving bad roads— Pillions —Beggars on every road—A squatter's turf cabin—Tea versus porridge and milk—Establishment of regular carriers—Farmers without vehicles—Peat and manure carried in panniers on donkey-back—Peat the only fuel of the "West of Ireland—Our kitchen arrangements—Rush-lights and "moulds"— 'What our housekeeping meant—I see a dying sheep—Our Christmas-boxes and " mummers "—Our butler—My friend the coachman—The pathetic story of our old nurse—Departing emigrants to America—Whiskey and " wailing"—Boxty bread,

I T WOULD BE difficult for any person visiting Ireland now, or, indeed, for the younger members of the present generation of Irishmen, to realise what the country was like when my father settled down in it in 1805, Brought up in Norfolk, he took great interest in farming, and he personally effected much for the temporal welfare of his poor parishioners by his example and teaching. Thus, the only ploughs known then in his district, or, indeed, in the "North of Ireland, were made of wood, primitive in construction, the share being just tipped with iron. With these the ground was merely scratched, the result being that the crop produced was of the poorest description.

My father got an iron plough down from Dublin, the advent of which excited the greatest wonder, mixed with admiration. He has told me of the crowds who would assemble to watch "the beautiful way she ploughed," and as a result not a few of the better class of farmers acquired similar ones. The wooden ploughs had entirely disappeared from out of our district before I was old enough to recollect them.

A tumbril cart, which arrived soon after the plough, was, however, not so well received, for many, not alone of the peasantry, but even of the gentry, clung to the old Irish carts then and for long after in general use. The wheels of these, which were quite common in my childhood, were not infrequently solid pieces of wood, often unshod, and sometimes the wheel and axle revolved together; and their load could never exceed a few hundredweight. The horses which drew them were wretched animals, and had to be unyoked to discharge the load. However, my father's kind, unobtrusive manner disarmed hostility, and by his example and teaching he effected a decided improvement amongst the poorer agriculturists.

He also succeeded in inducing the Grand Jury to improve the roads, which were shockingly bad. Our district was very hilly, and for the most part the roads ran from point to point direct, without any attempt at engineering.

I recently revisited the scenes of my childhood, and could hardly believe that I had often driven up and down hills on roads, since disused, which now seem to me to he dangerous even for equestrians to descend at a foot pace. I recollect the opening of a piece of new road, laid out by my father to cut off some of these terrible hills, which with no little difficulty he had persuaded the very conservative Grand Jury to make. How conservative these gentlemen were at that time may be guessed from the fact that the chief landowner in the parish, who was member of Parliament for the county, would never use the new portion of the road which led from his house to the church, but ordered his carriage always' to be driven over the old road, though this entailed stopping the carriage several times to put on and take off a slipper drag. He was an old general officer, who had served with distinction under Abercrombie in Egypt; He used to come to church regularly in a carriage drawn by four horses, with postillions and out-riders. I well remember his funeral, which by his special directions traversed the old road, the distance from his house to the Church being over three miles. With all his obstinate conservatism, he was a truly kind man, and good landlord; was, moreover, highly esteemed and on the most friendly terms with my father and mother.

Pillions were in common use during my childhood; not only did the women ride behind their brothers or husbands going to market, but also to church, to which a stable for the reception of the steeds was attached.

All this was long before the terrible potato famine of 1846-9, when the country was greatly over-populated by a mass of pauper and semi-pauper inhabitants. Beggars were met on every road and seen at every door; it, was a regular trade, and my father had to issue a kind of ticket, which he distributed to those who were supposed to reside inside the bounds of his parish. They were supposed not to be relieved at his house without producing this—a useless rule, as it in no way lessened the number of those who daily applied for alms at the hall door.

Then boys and girls of eighteen and nineteen married, without having any means of supporting themselves; often the pair would squat at the edge of a bog, building a one-roomed cabin of peat sods, and in this they passed their life and reared children, who, though barefooted and dirty, were always bright, and, like their parents, cheerful. They lived on potatoes, of which a patch could in general be grown on the adjoining waste. How they existed in these wretched cabins it is hard to conceive; in a year or so after its erection the cabin would generally have sunk to well nigh half its original height, the gables uneven, the roof sagged and grass-grown, the floor of soft earth sunken, and in wet weather the hollows in it full of mud. A few lean hens would generally be seen walking promiscuously in and out, sharing in the meals, the skins of the potatoes being thrown to them as the family fed. A basket of potatoes would be placed in the centre of the floor, around which the family sat. The hens roosted in the cabin at night. This is no fancy sketch, hundreds of times have I, as a boy, gone into such cabins, and witnessed such a scene. If the "boy"* was the son of a farmer who held a few acres of land, he would most likely be permitted to erect a cabin on the edge of the farm; and he might be given a plot of ground for potatoes, in return for which he would help the father in farm work. In either case the husband might earn a pittance as a labourer, and the wife a trifle by selling her eggs to dealers who attended the markets, but then the price of eggs would not be more than sixpence a dozen, even in winter. The spinning wheel was to be seen in every house, the yarn spun being sold to be woven by hand looms into coarse linen. The farmers paid labourers but sixpence a day as wages, with a dinner of potatoes, though in harvest time they might receive as much as a shilling a day!

The better class of farmers fared somewhat better; they would frequently have porridge for breakfast, and, as they kept a cow or cows, milk with it; but the dinner and supper would be of potatoes with butter-milk. On Sundays there would be, perhaps, boiled bacon and cabbage for dinner. But potatoes remained the staple food

---

*   The term "boy" at that date included—and in many districts in Ireland still does include—every unmarried male, no matter what his age might be.

of the peasantry. "We children in our games used to sing the following rhyme:—

> "Potatoes they are delicate food,
> I know not any half so good;
> And you can have them boiled or roast,
> Or any way you like them most."

And it really expressed the feeling of the population. They loved them.

Tea was a great luxury, its price being prohibitive— five shillings the pound; and sugar sixpence. Butter, on the other hand, was very cheap, sixpence in summer and eightpence in winter at most. Even in the houses of the gentry the servants would not be given tea, but would have porridge and milk for breakfast and supper; meat, of course, and potatoes for dinner. The housekeeper, cook, and, but not always, the butler, would probably have tea.

Well would it be for the present generation if the old diet was in vogue still; now tea is drunk to a most injurious extent by all classes, and instead of porridge and milk, servants and even the very poorest classes live on tea and bread, the flour used for the latter being deprived of its most nutritious parts and often greatly adulterated. To this injudicious diet we may, I think, fairly attribute, at least in part, the early loss of teeth which disfigures alike our town and country population; and possibly also the rapid spread of consumption and the allied diseases amongst the population of Ireland. The stamina of the whole population seems to have deteriorated greatly.

Railways were, of course, unknown, and the goods traffic was mainly carried on by a class of men known as "carriers," who started from Dublin in companies of a dozen or more, or in fewer numbers from Belfast or Londonderry, each man driving a two-wheeled cart drawn by 'one good horse, the ends of the shafts being always prolonged backwards, so as to project four feet behind. These carts travelled fifteen or twenty miles a day, and carried every conceivable kind of goods. Our house being situated near the road leading to Londonderry, the rattle of the carts could easily be heard, and often as a child did I listen to them as I lay m bed at night.

The journey between Dublin and Londonderry generally occupied them ten days, and the arrival of one of the carts at the glebe was an event to us children. I remember well one of them arriving in the yard having a gig, which my father had purchased in Dublin, perched on the top of a big load.

These carriers only served the towns and "villages on the main routes, and prior to 1815, when Bianconi started his first car, there was virtually no communication between places off the coach roads. Pedlars who carried their packs on their backs afforded to the poorer and, indeed, to many of the better-off the only means of supplying their wants. These men often visited our house in my childhood, and if I got the chance it was a treat to me to see their store of goods displayed. Among the traders of this class was the Italian, Charles Bianconi. He having obtained capital to the amount of one hundred pounds, started business, making the town of Clonmel his headquarters. He traversed the country for many miles round, carrying his goods himself. Feeling the great want of conveyances between the towns in the district in which he traded, he finally decided to start a one-horse car, to run daily between Clonmel and the neighbouring town of Caher, six miles distant. The experiment, as every one knows, was successful. This was in 1815. He soon started cars to ply to other towns in the neighbourhood. Then the one-horse cars, being inadequate to meet the traffic, he had long four-wheeled cars built to be drawn by two horses; and so he went on extending till, in 1845, he was working over 8,000 miles of roadway daily, Sundays always excepted. At the end of bis life he declared that this rule of his not to work his horses on Sundays, made in reverence to the day, paid well. He found that his horses not only did their work better from having the rest on the seventh day, but lasted so much longer, so as more than to counterbalance the money they would have earned by working on that day.

He made a fortune, and died universally respected at the age of ninety.

While the farmers had carts of a sort, and some of the

better-off realising in time the advantages of those used by my father would purchase such, the mass of the poorer class, tilling their little holdings of from one to three or four acres (the former being much the most numerous) had none at all, very many not as much as a wheelbarrow. They were contented to carry the manure, a heap of which was always to be seen close to the door of their cabin, to the field where the potatoes were to be grown, and the potatoes, when matured, to their dwelling in "creels," so constructed that, by withdrawing a peg, the bottom opened and allowed the little load of manure or potatoes to drop out at each side of the ass, or, it might be, half-starved pony, from whose sides the "creels" were suspended.

These petty farmers had seldom any other load to be carried except those and the peat for fuel from the bog, which was brought in like manner. But if a market town was not too far distant, the ass might be seen occasionally in company with many others, each laden with two creels full of peat fuel for sale, the value of the load being probably sixpence; but then there were but few who had fuel to spare, too often their little store of it being expended ere the winter was over. Coal was absolutely unknown in the inland districts of the North of Ireland. I never saw a coal fire till, when ten years old, I passed with my parents through Dublin, on our way to England.

Turf, as peat is always called in Ireland, is still the only fuel used by the poor throughout the West, and largely also in the central districts of Ireland, immense tracts in those localities being bog land. There is no coal of good quality in Ireland. Turf is cheap and in some respects a cleanly fuel, for though the large quantity of ash that remains after its combustion is very light and easily blown about, it does not soil as coal ashes do, and the smoke emitted while peat is burning is very different from that of coal, which blackens everything around.

But peat is quite unsuited for any house where there is much cooking and many fires going. In my father's house a lad was employed for hours every day in winter in carrying in from the "turf house" the needful supply. The kitchen fireplace, of course, was an open one, of great length. From a bar over it was suspended at one end a large boiler, a vessel with projecting cock; this was to supply the hot water used for all purposes except the making of tea, etc., and had to be refilled continuously by hand, for our Water supply was drawn from a well, situated much below the level of the house, and it had to be carted up daily in large barrels. In addition to the boiler, one or more kettles were always suspended on the bar over the fire, as well as pots for cooking, etc. Joints of meat, fowls, etc.; were roasted on a long spit, which, when in use, ran along the whole front of the fireplace and was turned by means of a "jack," an open frame, which seemed to me to be full of wheels and which was wound up when needed. This was an object of wonder to me in my childish days. The quantity of turf consumed in the huge fireplace was enormous, for a basketful would be reduced to ashes in no time. Under it was a pit to receive the ashes, and into this pit the fire was "raked" each night at bedtime. "Raking " consisted of placing four or five pieces of half-burnt turf in a hole made in the ashes under the grate. Over these were laid some pieces of unburnt turf and the whole covered with ashes. The peat would then smoulder for many hours, and in the morning, being placed in the grate, would quickly burn up, and a fire would soon be had. In like manner a few pieces of half-burnt turf would be carried to the dining or other rooms where fires were needed—remember matches were unknown. If by accident the "raked" turf went out, the only resource lay in the use of a flint and steel. With these sparks were struck, which, falling into the tinder-box, made the tinder smoulder; then thin slips of wood tipped with sulphur were held close to the tinder, and after much blowing they would blaze, and so, with the help of sticks, a fire would be lighted. All this was a troublesome job, especially in winter time, in the dark, there being no means of lighting a candle. It is no wonder that the failure of the "raked" fuel to keep alight all night was looked on by the whole household as a misfortune.

In case of illness "rush"-lights were used to keep a subdued light in the sick-room: the rushes were peeled, a narrow strip of the peel being left on one side to strengthen them. The pith, when dry, was then dipped in tallow; the rush-lights thus made would burn slowly for two or three hours. The very poor sometimes used these lights instead of candles, even tallow candles being above their means; but as a rule the whole family went to bed ere it was quite dark and rose correspondingly early.

Then we had "bog wood"; long lengths of fir trees, with which the land many centuries ago had been clad, were every year met with at depths of five, ten or more feet from the surface, while the turf were being cut in the spring. These, when dried and cut into suitable lengths and then split up, ignited rapidly and blazed gloriously. In the winter afternoons it was common for us to sit round the drawing-room or nursery fire, playing or even reading without the need of other lights.

Candles, indeed, were a serious item in the household economy. Dip-candles were used in the nursery and kitchen and in most rooms, except the drawing-room, dining-room and my father's study. They were bought in large quantities in the county town, fourteen miles off, and the use of snuffers was needed inces-santly to prevent them smoking. We children soon became experts in the use of the snuffers, and well do I remember the wrath I excited when, as sometimes happened, I snuffed out the candle. Mould candles used to be made in the house, and often have I watched the process. There was a regular frame, with shelves running across it, each shelf perforated with holes large enough to admit the metal mould till it sank to the collar. Then wicks made of twisted cotton were passed down from top to the lowest dependent part, the conical end, the small opening in this being then plugged and the melted grease poured in at the wide end; these candles, too, required frequent snuffing. Wax candles were, of course, to be had, but they were too expensive for us, and were only used on special occasions. "Composite" candles did not come into use till much later, to be superseded by those now called paraffin.

My mother was a regular Martha and a clever housekeeper, and needed to be so, for our home was to a great degree self-supporting. There was always a very large household; my mother had fourteen children, of whom ten – seven sons and three daughters – lived. Then there was a governess for the girls and a tutor for the boys, for my father had no leisure to devote to teaching. Nothing except groceries and such like were bought; the glebe land supplied potatoes and oats, from which meal for porridge was made. Even wheat was grown, and a sufficient quantity ground by means of a hand-mill placed in a loft, to supply wholemeal to make brown bread. Flour, however, had to be bought. The week's supply of bread was baked once a week in a brick oven. The household had become smaller before I passed out of the nursery, but at one time a sheep used to be killed nearly every week.

I happened by accident, while very young, to see a poor sheep just as it was dying, and the sight of the blood gave me such a shock that I cannot even to the present day see blood with-out a feeling of repugnance. In later years, when I had to perform operations of the greatest importance, occupying sometimes much over an hour, I became so absorbed in what I was doing that I seemed to myself unconscious of everything else; then bleeding, if it occurred, affected me in no way, but I always disliked looking on. The carting of the dried turf from the bog in summer, for the supply of our house was a big job. A great quantity Was needed for the kitchen, and when to this was added that used in sitting-rooms, nursery and bedrooms, throughout the house, an idea may be formed of the quantity to be stored each season, three large "turf houses" were filled to the very roof each year. The turf could only be drawn from the bogs in dry weather, as the tracks along which the carts had to go were impassable when wet, and the carts were consequently always clean and dry when employed in carrying the fuel. One of the great delights of my childhood was to watch the arrival of one of the carts, and then, as soon as the load was discharged, to climb into the vehicle and persuade the man to give me a drive; or, as I grew older, to drive the horse myself at a trot to the bog, which was nearly two miles off. Oh! delightful were these clandestine excursions! and how little did I think of the long run home!

I was a lonely child, the youngest of ten surviving. Five of my brothers were out in the world before I left the nursery; a sister and brother nearer my own age were at school; so games I had none, for I had no playfellow, but I was quite happy. I learned to ride before I can remember, and I recollect the delight of the winter on the ponds, for the frosts were certainly more severe and of longer duration seventy years ago than they are now. Christmas seemed a glorious time, but what my grand-children would think of the Christmas-boxes with which I was content, I can well imagine, for the nearest shop at which presents could be bought was fourteen miles off, and even then the choice was of the poorest kind. But then there was a splendid plum pudding as big as a small haycock; this would be carried in all aflame. There were mince pies, too, home-made cakes, etc., and for us youngsters a bottle of home-made gooseberry wine; whiskey was forbidden in my father's house, save for cooking purposes.

Then I have vivid recollections of bands of boys being admitted to the kitchen at Christmas time, dressed up fantastically to the best of their ability, and called "mummers"; and of the excitement of us children, when the servant would, some evening between Christmas and Twelfth Night, enter the drawing-room and utter the almost magic words, "The mummers have come." Down we would rush to find the kitchen cleared, the servants ranged round the wall, and the table brought to one end for us to stand on. These mummers were boys, farmers' and labourers' sons residing in the district, and were of course poorly clad, but decorated with scraps of coloured calico and ribbon sewed on here and there, and I think they wore paper caps of various shapes. They came into the kitchen one by one, each reciting some scrap of doggerel verse, and when the whole band had come in they danced in some fantastic way on the flagged kitchen floor. Then, a little money being given them, they went their way to some farmer's house, at which they might hope to receive a trifle. One of their rhymes has fixed itself in my memory, probably because it frightened me. A boy, aged about thirteen, father better got-up than the others, with a frying-pan in his hand, on one occasion entered, strutted into the centre of the floor, and turning to face us, Said,—

> "Here come I, little Devil Doubt;
> Under my arm I carry a clout;
> In my hand a dripping-pan;
> Money I want and money I crave,
> If you don't give me money, I sweep all to the grave."

These mummeries, like many other old customs, have disappeared since the famine years.

A butler whom we had, James MacIntosh by name, looms largely in the memory of my childhood. He was an active little man and full of fun. Before my brother went to school we used sometimes to be sent out for walks, under his supervision. These walks were delightful. James would not keep to the toad, but led us across fields and over ditches, and up to the top of high hills we would never have ventured to climb. Then he would make us play at being soldiers. We had some kind of a flag and marched to the music of a penny whistle. He moulded lead shillings, too, which we received as pay, they being duly returned to him to be paid out again on another occasion. Oh, what little things may make childhood happy!

When I was left alone on my brother's departure, James taught me to play battle door and shuttlecock, and I became quite expert at it. I would steal, too, into the dining-room as he was laying the table, and receive instruction in that art. I do not think I ever heard him use an improper word, but he told the funniest stories and had any number of doggerel lines and comical songs. One of the former is retained in my memory to the present day, and runs thus:—

> "A knife and a clod spells Nebby Cod,
> A knife and a razor spells Nebby Cod Nazer,
> One pair of boots and two pair of shoes
> Spells Nebby Cod Nazer the King of the Jews!"

What a wonderful thing is memory to retain such nonsense and forget things useful or entertaining! Poor man! I only saw him once after I went to school. He called at my house some twenty years later; he was still in service, but looked old and shabby. I fear that, like many old servants, he was on the downward grade. I have never forgotten him.

The coachman was another friend. He was a staid man of about forty, who had been in my father's service before I was born. He taught me to ride before I can remember. One ride made a great impression on me. I cannot have been, at the most, more than eight years old, if so much. It was impressed on my memory by two incidents. One was, that as we rode past some urchins who stood on the road side, one of them asked if I "was tied on." This I considered an insult. I was perched on a mare belonging to my sister, which must have been quite fourteen and a half hands high, the coachman holding a rein to control her if she became frisky; otherwise I was independent; the other, that we rode down to the shore of the lake where it was level and the water shallow, and the coachman made me ride into the water till the horses were knee deep. This at first frightened and then delighted me.

Our old nurse's story was a rather pathetic one. She had married a soldier about the year 1810. Soon after the birth of a son he was ordered off to the wars and she returned to service, hearing from him only at long intervals, the last authentic news being that he was with his regiment at Waterloo. His name, however, did not appear in the lists of those killed or wounded, and finally he was reported "missing" and never again was heard of. After the lapse of several years she married my father's right-hand man, who superintended the men who worked on the glebe lands, which were extensive, bought cattle, killed sheep, etc.; he was a good deal younger than the nurse, They were settled in the gate lodge before I can remember, and it was a great resort of mine.

Daily used I to run down there, delighted to watch her spinning the flax, as did also her servant, a young woman, who would tell me wondrous stories, mainly fairy tales. One was specially interesting about a fairy who, assuming the form of a bull-calf, carried off on his back through the air a child who had " sneezed three times without any one saying, "God bless you." This story frightened me much, lest the like should happen to me!

Well, for years the pair lived happily. Then from the blue came the bolt. The husband had been sent to a fair by my father, but instead of returning sent a letter to say that he had gone off to America, and, as we soon learned, had taken with him the young wife of a carpenter who had recently settled in the neighbourhood, and whose husband had, it appeared, accompanied them. America was then a far distant land, from which few ever returned.

My father allowed the poor woman to remain in the lodge and so things went on for more than a year, when one afternoon, hearing some one at the door, she went to it to find her husband propped up against it, powerless to move without help. It appeared that he had a paralytic stroke soon after reaching America. Then, when his money was spent, becoming a burthen on the pair, they brought him back and left him derelict at his wife's door. She took him in and nursed him tenderly till death came to release him, which was not until a year and a half later.

It was at about this time (1885-6) that emigrants began to go to America—at first, few in number and at long intervals. The probable departure of a young man, or of a whole family, would be the talk of the country for months beforehand, Londonderry was the usual place of embarkation for our part of the country. When the time arrived for the departure of the emigrants there was invariably a gathering of friends and neighbours on the previous evening to testify their sorrow by getting up a festive entertainment. At this gathering, though tea was generally to be had, whiskey was the beverage which was most freely forthcoming and most freely imbibed. Nearly every guest was sure to bring a bottle of it. The conviviality was kept up all night, but the grief, which was chiefly manifested by the loudest wailings, was reserved till the hour arrived when the emigrants must leave their old home. The crowd followed them for miles, and the wailing could be heard long after all were out of sight.

Some one composed a ballad descriptive of the festive

scene. I have forgotten all of it, save two lines, describing the powers of consumption of food and the after-effects on a guest who

> "Eat scones of Boxty bread
> And oceans drank of tea."

Boxty bread was made of equal parts of raw potatoes grated, and flour; was baked on a griddle; was heavy and indigestible. Each scone would weigh quite one pound. The ballad described the subsequent suffering and the cure, which consisted of rolling and rubbing, and whiskey administered freely.

CHAPTER III

TRAVELLING IN PRE-RAILWAY TIMES AND SCHOOL LIFE SEVENTY YEARS AGO

A journey from Ireland to Norwich—"The game of the road"—A wretched crossing—A short cut not always ihe shortest way— Hospitality of the Norfolk people—Three meals within three hours—My first Cricket—The wretched little steamer—The terrible storm of 1839— "The great wind"— I go to school at Maidstone, Kent—A very roundabout way to get there— My school and some schoolfellows—The Incident of the broken windows— First postage stamps— Maidstone Fair—The tragic story of one of my schoolfellows—The Japanese assassin.

WHEN I was ten years old my father and mother visited Norfolk for the first time in their married life. My eldest brother had married and was residing in the old family mansion, Brandiston Hall, some nine miles from Norwich. This journey was an event in my life. The party consisted of my parents, two sisters, an infant grandchild, the latter's nurse, and myself. The whole of the inside of the coach to Dublin, and that from Manchester to Norwich, was engaged several days beforehand, as also an outside seat.

We stayed the first night at a friend's house situated on

the coach road, some miles on the Dublin side of Enniskillen so we did not join the coach till after seven o'clock. At nine the coach stopped for half an hour for breakfast at a little country inn; that breakfast was an amazing treat for me, and afterwards great was my delight when for a time I was permitted to sit outside with my sister, and see the coachman whip up the horses, and the guard behind, clad in a red coat, blowing the horn as we passed through villages or entered a town, That guard was a character. I came to know him well in after years. He used to amuse us boys as we travelled to school with his wonderful stories, and he taught us "the game of the road." He took one side of the road, and we the other, while we counted who would make, say, 100 first: men did not count, but every woman, cow, sheep or pig we passed on our respective sides of the road, or in the fields adjacent, counted each so much. I think a pig gained the highest number—five, a sheep or a woman one each, and so on. When the weather was fine these journeys on top of a coach were delightful, but in wet weather horrible. We had no waterproofs in those days, no rugs, and if one had an old coat to throw over his knees he was well off. Umbrellas were of little use; indeed, on a real wet day the drip off them only added to one's discomfort. I have been wet through before the coach stopped for breakfast, sat in that state in heavy rain till after dark, and been none the worse for it; but then I was young and hardy in those days, when luxurious travelling was unknown. The crossing by steamer to Liverpool, which was then the mail route, and which occupied from twelve to fourteen hours, was a wretched experience. I was very ill, too ill to care for any breakfast at the hotel in Liverpool but the excitement of the railway journey to Manchester, the line having been opened not long before, and being still a wonder, revived me.

We slept in Manchester, starting early next morning on the two days' journey across England to Norwich. Of that Journey I only remember two events—namely, what seemed to me the splendid dinner we had at the inn, somewhere in Derbyshire, at which the coach stopped at midday; and the hotel in Newark where "the coach slept." My belief now is that the dinner consisted of merely roast mutton and potatoes, etc.; but at the time I thought otherwise of it, and I was very hungry. The coach did not reach Norwich till near sunset on the second day, and it became dark ere we reached Brandiston. We had, too, an adventure on the way, for my brother, thinking to take a short cut, turned down a narrow little-used by-road, to find after a time it was the wrong one, and, it being too narrow to permit of the carriage being turned with the horses attached, we had all to get out in the dark and have them and the pole, too, taken out, ere we could get round. That was my first experience of Norfolk and its "ways.".

My next experience was an illustration of the hospitality of the Norfolk people. The greater part of the small estate which descended to my father was rented to one of those gentlemen farmers who did so much to uphold the reputation of England before she became well nigh a mere manufacturing centre, and who were ruined by the repeal of the corn laws. Well, we were all invited to tea at his house, and of course went. We arrived before five o'clock, and almost immediately afterwards adjourned to the dining-room, where before my delighted eyes I saw all kinds of good things spread on the table to which I did ample justice. My father then took me with him to be shown the farm buildings, horses, pigs, etc. We were back in less than an hour, when we were told tea was ready! I thought we had had it, but on entering the parlour for the second time was astonished to find that the former repast was only light refreshment. It appeared we had been expected an hour earlier. The "tea" consisted of much more than that beverage. There were hot cakes and cold cakes, and every variety of home-made sweets. I deeply regretted that I had not known what was to come when I had indulged so freely at the preceding repast, but I managed to get down a good lot of the delicious fare.

Then, it being still daylight, we went for a stroll over the farm. I saw what Norfolk farming in those days meant. Large fields of ripe grain, of turnips, etc., in long rows, without a weed visible, and the plants exactly the same distance apart, and so on; for this was the time when high-class farming was at its zenith in England.

Returning to the house, my mother, after a time, rose to say goodbye, to be told that could not be, for supper was just ready—a third meal inside three hours! And what a supper was this! hot meats, cold meat pies, pastry, and what not! Alas, alas! that supper was virtually lost to me; there was no room left into which I could pack more. Alas, too, that the prosperous, generous English farmers of this class, so well portrayed by Dickens, are extinct! While at Brandiston I was initiated into the art of bait fishing for carp and other small fry in a pond in the grounds. My taste for this sport has never been quite lost. In like manner I saw cricket—a game then unknown in Ireland —played for the first time, and I too played with other boys. Later on I was proficient in the game in a small way, and retain an interest in it to the present day.

Our return journey was even more tedious than the outward one. We went from Norfolk to Harrogate on account of my father's health. There being no railway, and the coach journey to Yorkshire a tedious and roundabout one, all of us, except my mother, went by sea from Yarmouth to Hull, and on to Goole, where we transhipped to a canal boat, and then on by coach to Harrogate. The sail from Yarmouth to Goole, we were told, would occupy some six or eight hours; in point of fact we were more than twenty-six hours in that wretched little steamer, which I now know was about the size of a small tug, and, oh! how sick I and everyone else, except my father, were! There was but one little cabin with four berths round it, so the floor was covered with sick men, women and children. My sisters fortunately were well enough to remain on deck with my father, till, at about 10 p.m., when we anchored somewhere off Grimsby in shelter, and some plan made for sleeping, my sisters, I know, got berths.

The winter of 1838-9 was memorable on account of the terrible storm which occurred in January, 1839. I was the only child in the house, and slept in my father's dressing-room. In the middle of the night I was awakened by my father coming in, lifting me out of bed and carrying me to my mother's room. I then learned that the window of the room in which I slept had been smashed by slates which had been whirled off the roof, carried like leaves by the wind and dashed against it. My father and the butler remained up all night, as indeed did the women servants, who all congregated in the kitchen. The house, strongly built though it was, rocked, but resisted the storm; half the roof was torn off. In the morning the lawn was seen to be covered with slates, most of them sticking upright on the ground, as a quoit would. Large trees were uprooted, and acres of young plantations on the glebe lands levelled. Even the cottages of the poor suffered terribly. One poor man climbed on to the roof of his cabin, which was situated on the shore of Lough Erne, a few miles from our house, to place heavy stones on the thatch, in the vain hope of saving the roof, when a terrible gust swept the whole roof, and the man on it, right into the lake, where the man was drowned.

In Dublin the terrors of the night were augmented by the burning rafters from the roof of the Bethesda school-house, which had taken fire, being carried by the wind considerable distances. Slates and brickwork fell in all directions. It was the most disastrous storm Ireland has experienced, and to the present day, in the North of Ireland at any rate, 1889 is still spoken of with awe as the year of "The Great Wind."

That winter was a severe one; there was much snow and severe frost. I recollect the delightful sliding on the smooth ice, the successful snaring of blackbirds and thrushes, and the rich harvest of snipe and woodcock the sportsmen made. It was a memorable winter to me, the more so as it was the last whole winter I ever spent at home. Summer saw me going with my brother to the Grammar School, Maidstone, Kent, where he had been for some time.

How well I remember the journey there—the start on a lovely summer morning before 4 a.m. the long, delightful day on top of the coach; the arrival at the old schoolhouse, long since abandoned for newer and better quarters; my abject terror at finding myself left alone amongst what seemed to me a crowd of boys—I who had lived such a secluded life, almost companionless! But that soon wore off. I fear I was somewhat pugnacious, for I know I went to church with a black eye my very first Sunday there. It was given me by another Irish boy, and no doubt very well deserved.

It now seems strange that my parents chose a school so far away, at a time when travelling was so tedious, for the London and Birmingham Railway was not then completed, and our first journey to school was a round-about one. We went most of the way by coach from Manchester to Hull, the railway being open only to Rochdale; from Hull to Gravesend by steamer, the voyage occupying twenty-four hours; and thence by omnibus through Chatham to Maidstone. At Chatham there was a delay of an hour or so, and my brother left me at the inn while he went off to see some friends he had in the town. Left by myself, I ventured to order a bottle of gingerbeer, which the waiter duly brought and was proceeding to open when I stopped him, saying I would do so myself. This I deferred doing till he left the room; then, not knowing how to do it, the cork flew out unexpectedly, and away went the gingerbeer all over the tablecloth; the loss of that drink was great, but that was nothing compared to my terror. I must have expected some retri-bution would follow, for to the present day I remember my joy at the waiter making nothing of the accident and quickly sopping up the mess I had made.

I spent two years happily enough at Maidstone. The school was a small one—there were about thirty boarders; but what would the present generation of schoolboys think if they went home but once a year, as was the fate of several of us. The journey from the North of Ireland to Kent was so long and so expensive that we, and a few other Irish boys, had to spend the Christmas holidays at school; and there was no Easter vacation in those days at any school. We, however, were very contented, and, indeed, happy, during the vacations; not that we did not long for home, but then the delight of returning there when the summer came round was great. The master, Mr. Harrison by name, was kind to us. We were quite free to go in and out, into the town or to the country, as we liked. We were invited to the drawing-room of an evening pretty frequently, when he and his wife would join in games of cards, such as "Pope Joan," "Commerce," or other round games, which seem long since to have fallen into oblivion. When alone, we used to play whist for hours at a time, but once the school term commenced we never touched a card.

Mr. Harrison was not only a kind-hearted man, but was a good master; certainly he trained us to be truthful. For example, on one occasion a squabble took place in the small enclosed playground attached to the school between a lot of us little boys and some of the big ones; and as we could not fight them with our fists, we pelted them with cabbage stalks, a heap of which we discovered in the garden close at hand. Now the schoolroom and dining-hall had once been parts of an old monastery, and were lighted by large Gothic windows which looked on the playground. Our missiles generally missed the chap we aimed at, not a few struck the wall, and occasionally one landed in a window, smashing' glass, and, worse, breaking the lead in which the little diamond-shaped panes were inserted. At any rate, one aimed by me at the head of a big boy missed him, landed in a window, and smashed a lot of these panes, making a great hole. This catastrope helped to cool our ardour, and the battle ended by our running away.

Next morning the handsome windows were seen to be in a sad plight, and I believe we were all very sorry for what had happened, unintentionally on our part, and we all expected to be punished. The course, however, that Mr. Harrison took was to announce that all pocket-money was stopped till each boy stated how many panes of glass he had broken—bear in mind these were small diamond-shaped panes, such as are seen in the windows of many old churches. A list was accordingly made out, which I headed, acknowledging to the smashing of a dozen or so of panes, all smashed by that one unlucky shot, which had been seen by all; but by a strange coincidence, not one of the other small boys could be found who had broken more than two; most of them would acknowledge to one only. Well, the list went in at one o'clock, just before dinner.

No sooner was dinner over than a message came ordering me to attend in the study. I was, of course, greatly frightened, and my comrades cheered me by telling me I must stuff copy books up my sleeves and inside my vest to deaden the blows of the cane I should be thrashed with. I was a very small boy, even for my age, which was just twelve, and Mr. Harrison was very tall and big in proportion. In terror I entered the study; he was standing in the middle of the room clad as in school time, in cap and gown, wearing his large, gold-rimmed spectacles and holding the list in his hand. He at once addressed me sternly, saying, "You have broken all these panes of glass?"

I replied, almost crying, that I did not intend to do it, and that some of them had previously been cracked.

"I don't care for that," he said as sternly as before; then, changing his tone, added, "You are the only boy in the school who has told the truth. Here," he added, putting half a crown in my hand; "keep that till I ask for it, and come in and dine with us to-day."

I have never forgotten that lesson, or ceased to honour the old man's memory.

Letters in those days were few and far between, for as the postage on every letter we received from home, in the North of Ireland, was two shillings and ninepence, and the reply cost the same, expense having to be considered we received only one and wrote one home every month. The penny postage came into use in 1840, during my first year at that school. It was a great boon. I have recently given my grandchild one of the first stamps issued, taken off a letter of ours to my mother, which I found after her death, and which, no doubt, was posted by me that year.

The two years' school life at Maidstone were happy ones; we had a good deal of liberty, and in summer fished for perch, carp, etc., in the Medway. One day I well remember, when my brother and I returned bearing three dozen small perch, to us a wonderful event; my share was caught with a rod purchased with the half-crown the master had given me for telling the truth. Then we were occasionally allowed to go in a boat on the river with a master, and Wednesdays and Saturdays being half-holidays we played cricket in summer on an adjoining common, now, I believe, enclosed. Lessons gave us but little trouble. I learned the rudiments of Latin and Greek without difficulty, and I did not realise till I went to another school the wretchedness of being overdriven in lesson work.

The annual fair, held in May on waste ground lying between the school and river, was a great event in our school life. We were allowed to visit it during certain hours. I had never seen such a sight before, and was delighted. There was a menagerie, of course, peep shows,

Punch and Judy, Aunt Sally in various forms, and other such means of beguiling little boys and tempting them to get rid of their pennies. But the cheap-jacks were what captivated me most, and the wonderful way articles cheapened down. You saw, say, a penknife handed over for sixpence, for the exact counterpart of which you yourself or someone else had been enticed to give a shilling a few minutes before! The system of these cheap-jacks was to produce an article, say a knife, and, standing on the step of the van, call out, "Who will bid for this splendid article? Who will have it for two and sixpence?"

There being no bid the man would rapidly reduce the sum named, saying, "Well, we will say two and fourpence, two and two, two shillings; will none give two shillings for this first-class knife?"

Still no response, and the cheapening went on till someone would perhaps buy it when it came to one and two or a shilling, and it was handed to him.

Instantly another identical article was put up at the price the previous one had fetched, and a purchaser often would appear; if not, the price would in general descend again with marvellous rapidity till it reached the actual value of the article, when, if bidders did not appear, that article was withdrawn, and another of quite a different kind produced.

I used to watch these cheapjacks for, I am sure, an hour at a time, and I wonder if such scenes still occur at the English country fairs? The cheapjacks evidently made a good thing of it, for, besides us schoolboys, maidservants, yokels and the country girls who would be with them were easy victims to their wiles.

That fair is a thing of the past. I visited Maidstone a few years since to find the fair green converted into a well-kept concreted cattle market, and the school itself into a hop store. For a trifling tip I gained access to the dormitory in which I used to sleep, and saw a huge pocket of hops occupying the space my bedstead formerly stood on. I was glad to find the school flourishing on a new and better site.

I well remember all the talk about the marriage of Queen Victoria with Prince Albert, which took place in February, 1840; and subsequently the birth of the Princess Royal. Both events occurred while I was at Maidstone, and gave us half-holidays.

Another matter which kept us boys in a state of excitement was watching for news of the "President" steamship; we watched in vain. At that time steam navigation was in its infancy, and the "President" was one of the few steamers which had ventured to cross the Atlantic; she had on board Power, a celebrated actor. Of that ill-fated ship, of crew or passengers, no sign or tidings have ever been heard.

One or two of my schoolfellows at the grammar school were my friends in after-life. One of these, a boy of my own, age, to whom I was much attached, had a sad fate. His name was Baldwin, and he was almost friendless. His mother was dead, and his father, a captain in the 31st Regiment, was in India; the boy hardly remembered him, for he had hot seen him since early childhood. Baldwin was in the charge of the master and his wife, and seemed to have no relatives, for he never went anywhere for vacation. On the whole he was kindly treated by Mr. and Mrs. Harrison, but was more or less neglected. His pocket-money was very scanty and clothes often shabby. He was very clever at school work, but erratic and untidy. His name was down for admission to Woolwich, for which he was to be prepared when older.

As a lieutenant his father had been present with his regiment at Waterloo; subsequently he was on board the "Kent, East Indiaman," when that ship took fire in the Indian Ocean and when, by the exercise of the most perfect discipline, the soldiers, passengers and crew were saved and taken on board a small brig, the " Cambria," of 500 tons, which fortunately hove in sight. But Mr. Baldwin unfortunately had his leg lacerated by a piece of iron while climbing the side of the brig. In India he obtained his company, but there his promotion stopped, for the old purchase system was in force and he had no money to purchase the next step. Thus the lieutenant who had gone through the perils of Waterloo was still only a captain in 1841, and so remained till the first Sikh war broke out in 1845. The 31st were then sent to the front. In Lord Gough's first action, one of the field officers of the regiment being killed, Captain Baldwin obtained his majority without purchase, only to lose his life in the bloody battle of Ferozebad a few weeks later.

The news of his father's long-waited-for promotion and of his death reached his son almost simultaneously. The latter was then a cadet at Woolwich, much to his own surprise, for at that time interest was all-powerful and candidates for admission to the Academy who were without powerful friends would be passed over, in favour of others who had influence. Indeed, the friendless candidate would often not be called to appear at the examination for admission till past the age limit.

Baldwin, finding he was approaching the limit of age without being summoned, gave up all hope of obtaining admission to the Academy, and was preparing for a university when he was unexpectedly called up. He made a brilliant examination and was, of course, admitted, but he was not happy there. He had but a small allowance, ill-fitting clothes, and was wanting in polish; he was therefore delighted to find himself gazetted as Ensign, without purchase, in his father's old regiment, the 81st, in the ranks of which there were many vacancies after the bloody campaign it had passed through. His father, it appeared, had got his name down for a commission when he thought that his son had no chance of gaining admission to Woolwich; and the Horse Guards made the tardy reparation for their neglect of the father by at once giving the cadet a commission. He was received with a welcome on joining the 31st in which his father had served so long, and became popular. The regiment soon returned from India, and in 1850. was quartered in Dublin, where I had just settled, and I was delighted to have my old schoolfellow at my house. Then came the Crimea war, and he went there with his regiment, served through the whole campaign without once seeking leave, and attained the rank of captain before he was twenty-five.

On his return to England he was one of the first to join the Staff College just then instituted. He passed through it successfully, and shortly after obtained his majority.

Then once more for a few hours he came into our life; for, being appointed to some post on the staff of the Commander-in-Chief, he was sent down to inspect the Norfolk rifle corps, one of the numerous bodies of volunteers which were formed after the conclusion of the Crimea war. My brother, who, like myself, had been his schoolfellow, was at that time Deputy Chief Constable of Norfolk, and was told off to command the escort of mounted police in attendance on the Prince and Princess of Wales, who came down to be present at the inspection. So my brother came in contact with Major Baldwin. I recollect receiving a letter from my brother telling me how he had ridden beside the Princess of Wales, then recently married, and how surprised he was to recognise in the staff officer who inspected the corps his old schoolfellow Baldwin.

Being anxious to see foreign service. Major Baldwin soon after exchanged into a regiment quartered in India. Just then our relations with Japan had become strained. The British Residency had been attacked, and the Queen's representative, Sir Rutherford Alcock's life endangered. Troops were ordered up from India, and amongst them George Baldwin's regiment. Peace was patched up and there was no fighting, but the people were intensely hostile, and foreigners were warned that the roads were not safe.

Notwithstanding the warning, Baldwin and his friend, Lieutenant Bird, determined to visit a temple some miles distant. When nearing the place, they were suddenly attacked from behind by men armed with two-handed swords. The first blow, struck from behind, clove Baldwin's head right down to the neck; that aimed at Bird glanced off the skull and nearly severed the shoulder from the body; he lived a few hours, just long enough to be able to tell the tale. So ended the lives of two promising officers; Baldwin, in fact, was already a distinguished man. The news of his death shocked and distressed me greatly. I had a great regard for my old schoolfellow.

CHAPTER IV

MY IRISH SCHOOL

The headmaster's object in life—All classics—Caning—We have play hour but no games—I am always behindhand—The curriculum —No French or German—Our objectionable dormitories—Our washing bowls—Food plentiful and good, but—— —Tablecloth but no plates for breakfast— I start a cricket club and issue a challenge—The moral standard of our school was low—The under-masters—I am apprenticed to a doctor and pass my examinations.

AFTER THE SUMMER vacation of 1841, my brother went up to the university, and my parents, thinking it better I should not be so far from home, transferred me from Maidstone to an Irish school, supposed to be the best in the country, a reputation resting wholly on the fact that pupils from it obtained very frequently first place at the entrance examinations for Trinity College, Dublin. For this they were very carefully prepared— indeed, crammed. To me the change from the English school was great, and it certainly did not make for my happiness. The school I now went to was a comparatively large one, there being some 120 boarders and 60 day boys. With the latter the boarders did not associate; they were not allowed into the playfields, and had to leave the premises the moment the schoolwork ceased.

The headmaster certainly was a remarkable, if narrow-minded man; he did his duty to the best of his judgment, and lived for his school. His one object in life was to see his pupils' names in the honour lists, and to attain this he never spared himself. He was in the schoolroom (and there was but one room for the 180 boys) from 7.30 a.m., summer and winter, till 3 p.m. when school was over, except, of course, the interval of about an hour and a half, between nine and ten-thirty o'clock for breakfast and washing, which latter was not expected to be done by the boys before breakfast. Out of school hours we never saw him; his only recreation was a constitutional walk.

Rather under middle height, of a very spare figure, always wearing a tightly buttoned frock coat, with his sharp, clean-shaved face, you could not pass him unnoticed; but his ideas of education were limited to a degree. He evidently believed that every boy could be made a classical scholar, and that Latin and Greek were the only subjects really worthy of being taught, so the boys who could not master these subjects with facility had a wretched life. They were pronounced "idle" and punished accordingly. The assistant masters were not allowed to inflict any punishment; they reported all boys whose work was bad to him during school hours, and the ones so reported would be called up to the doctor's desk, and caned vigorously on the hands. These canings occurred frequently every day.

In addition to being caned, most of the boys so reported were ordered to remain in during the next play hour and learn the lesson. Then there were always the same three or four boys reported every day, for nearly every lesson; these, regularly from the end of the first week or so from the commencement of the term, would be ordered to remain in and work at their tasks during the whole of the play hours till that term ended. No doubt these boys generally were dullards, who seemed incapable of learning Greek and Latin; but one, whom I remember well to have been a bright little fellow, was one who, under different treatment, should have done well. He, term after term, was kept in, not having one hour for recreation in the day. The system was an awful one, and though, no doubt, a few of the pupils became good classical scholars, I only know of one of my schoolfellows who attained even moderate eminence in after-life.

My own case was a curious one. At Maidstone, after reading a book or so of Caesar and then Ovid for a while, we were put into Virgil. Our lesson was a short one, for we were only beginners, and we had to prepare but six or eight lines for each lesson. At the end of the first week at this work the headmaster called the class up and announced that he was "going to teach us to scan." How well I remember that lesson! I can, even now, after the lapse of well nigh seventy years, repeat the line he took for his purpose; *Hic aliud majus miseris multoque tremendum.*—Virgil, Book II., line 119. He kept us before his desk for a full hour after the school had been dismissed, and so thorough was his instruction, that I never had further trouble in scanning such Latin verse as Virgil wrote.

Well, on going to the Irish school, the Doctor asked what book I was reading? I said, "Virgil." Then, without asking me another question, he desired me to go into the "Virgil class." I soon discovered that most of the boys in that class were not only from one to two years older than myself, but also beyond me in classical knowledge, and the amount of work to be prepared was three time's as much as I had been accustomed to. As a result I was always behindhand. The Greek work, in like manner, was beyond me. But this did not seem to have occurred to the Doctor. I did my very best, gave up much of my playtime to preparation in vain. I was pronounced "idle," caned, and, specially during my first year, "kept in" frequently.

Another peculiarity of the system was that there was no promotion of the boys at the head of a form to the one above them, so, except when a new boy happened to be put into the class, there was no change made. From the time I joined till I left the school three years later I was in the same form. Having read the six books of Virgil, we went on to Horace, then to Juvenal and the Latin plays in succession. Our work was increased, that was all; and the same with Greek—Xenophon. Homer, Greek plays, etc., indeed, every book named in the curriculum for the entrance examination of the University of Dublin. Having read these through, we began again. I went over most of them two or three times, so when I went up for the entrance examination I knew these books nearly off by heart; but my knowledge of the Greek and Latin languages was poor enough, and yet the school had the reputation of being a "splendid one"!

The result of this system was, that one or two boys who were always at the top of the class gained high places at entrance, and classical Honours in the University course; but the rest of the class learned little. English was hardly taught at all, just a little history (and that ancient), and geography: indeed, the latter was a mere form. Not a single boy learned French or German. Mathematics were relegated to a secondary place, and counted for little in school work; this was unfortunate for me, for Euclid and algebra gave me no trouble, while I never succeeded in learning Greek properly. The only thing I really gained by my three years at that school was "application." I learned to give my attention to my work. My education, properly so-called, only began after I entered college. I virtually from that date educated myself, for I never had the help of a private tutor either in classics or medicine.

I believe I must have been one of those boys eager to acquire knowledge, but to whom such a routine as existed in that Irish school was destructive. I know I was incapable of retaining in memory Greek and Latin rules or verses, as being to me unaccompanied by any intellectual meaning. All my after-life I have regretted that the years devoted to learning a mere smattering of Greek were not devoted to learning German and French.

In other respects, also, the arrangements of the school were objectionable, the dormitories were very large, the smallest containing twenty, the largest as many as forty beds. "No basins or jugs were allowed in the dormitories, and the lavatory, such as it was, was situated below the level of the ground, being virtually a flagged cellar. Along its sides were benches, in which were cut circular spaces holding wooden bowls to be used as basins. On the floor in front of them lay a thick plank on which we stood, and which was always saturated with moisture. In the centre of the floor were tubs full of water. When a boy wanted to wash his face or hands, he took one of the wooden bowls, as likely as not full of dirty water left by the last user. This he emptied on the floor, which sloped towards a large opening under the one window which lighted the place; then, stepping off the plank, he filled the basin by dipping it into the tub, and proceeded with his ablutions.

No light was allowed in the lavatory in winter and for the first two winters I was there I regularly washed in the dark, feeling along till I got an empty basin and filling it as best I could, in the dark winter mornings, out of a tub. In general, I was alone, even when the mornings were brighter, for only some five or six boys out of the whole school washed before breakfast; they were not expected to do so. During my last winter at this school this vile arrangement was altered, a proper lavatory erected, water laid on, and light supplied during the dark winter mornings.

The arrangements for meals were nearly as primitive as those for washing. The food was plentiful and wholesome—this I am glad to be able to say—but what the present generation of schoolboys would think of it is another matter.

Morning school lasted from 7.30 a.m., summer and winter, till nine o'clock; then we trooped to the dining-hall for breakfast. The meal was served on long tables along each side of which were placed forms. Some forty boys sat at each table. Down the middle of the table were placed japanned bread baskets, filled with hunks of dry bread, each loaf having been cut into about a dozen square pieces, a large mug of milk being placed for each boy, cold in summer, hot or cold, as wished for, in winter. Knives and plates there were none, but the tablecloth was generally clean. Such was the invariable breakfast.

The boys reassembled for school at ten o'clock; and remained in the classroom till three, except on Wednesdays and Saturdays, when we broke up at 2 p.m. Every day at one the butler appeared in the schoolroom, carrying in front of him a large tray, on which were piled thick slices of dry bread, of which each of us took a slice as the man passed backwards and forwards between the rows of desks in front of which we sat; this was our lunch. Dinner was at five and consisted of joints of roast and boiled meat on alternate days, and of potatoes served in their skins. These we peeled ourselves, the skins lying in a heap on the cloth beside our plates. We had plenty to eat, and the meat was always good; but of vegetables, other than potatoes, we had none. Puddings were unheard of. Supper at eight o'clock was breakfast repeated, only that there never was any hot milk. Further, the school was a veritable jail, for no boy was permitted on any pretext, except a friend or relative called for him, to go outside the school premises.

It is but right that I should add that a few years after I had left the school a new master was appointed, a man of enlightened views as well as a capable master. He changed the entire system, remodelled the school on the lines of English public schools, and under him and his successors it has attained a high standard of excellence and is highly thought of.

Perhaps even more remarkable is the fact that no games were instituted. No doubt there was a fives court, but only one. Cricket was quite unknown, and neither football nor hockey were played. The senior boys deemed such games derogatory to their dignity, and no master took the least trouble to encourage games. We spent our spare time wandering aimlessly about the playfields, which were extensive.

In the summer, however, of 1842, I started the idea of getting up a cricket club. Out of the 120 boarders there were only myself and one other boy who knew anything of the game, or, in point of fact, had ever seen a game played. This boy was one of the seniors, a son of the then Recorder of Dublin, the late Sir Frederick Shaw. He undertook to organise a club to be composed of the older boys, and I one for the juniors. My scheme proved the more successful—partly because there were more of us, but mainly because boys thirteen or fourteen years of age took up the game more seriously and were more anxious to learn it.

But the ground was atrocious, and we received no help whatever from the master. In fact, he took no notice of us at all. All the same, we juniors practised zealously, and at the end of the season challenged the seniors to play a match, they to omit Shaw from their eleven. We beat them handsomely. To me this was the great event in my school life. Of course I was captain of the eleven. I had taught them all they knew of the game, and, as I bowled pretty well, took many wickets. At that date cricket was hardly known in Ireland, and not at all in the North. As far as I know, mine was the first attempt made to introduce it there. I believe the club ceased to exist after I left; but I visited the old school a few years ago, and, though it was during the vacation, I saw with pleasure the level, well-kept cricket ground where had been a rough field, all hills and hollows, in my day.

But I hated the school. It was a veritable jail. As I have already said, we were never permitted to go outside the playfields on any pretext, unless a relative or friend came for us. The headmaster's principle seemed to be that no boy was to be trusted in the smallest degree; consequently nothing was gained by being well conducted, and it is not to be wondered at that his precautions failed to keep up the moral standard of the school. Bad language was common amongst the boys to a terrible extent, and you would constantly hear shocking oaths and profane speech.

Much of this was, without doubt, due to the class of men who were assistant masters, for with the exception of the senior of these, who was a charming old man, and whose memory I still hold in esteem, and one other, who was well intentioned, but incompetent, all were unworthy of trust. One specially, I remember—who was a prime favourite with the headmaster, because, being very sharp, he found out and reported trifling misde-meanours, many of which had best been unnoticed, and in other ways curried favour —was unprincipled to a degree. He watched like a hawk any boy whom he knew the headmaster did not view with favour; while he winked at, and in truth connived at, the grossest misconduct of those with whom he chose to be friends. I at the time believed, and still believe, that he must have even connived at one or two of his favourites getting out at night into the town. I believe, too, that he knew that whiskey was brought in by them, and that it was introduced into the school by other means. His bed was arranged at the extremity of a large dormitory in which I slept during my last term at school. One night I was awakened by someone fumbling at the door. I got up and opened it to admit this master so drunk that he with great difficulty reached his bed. What could be expected of a school with such men as masters?

A somewhat serious attack of illness sent me home not long after this occurrence, and I resolved that I would not go back. I had always a great desire to be a physician, but I had a horror of the sight of blood; but being told that I must be familiar with surgery, even though I never were to practice it, I had given up the idea. Now, however, my determination not to return to school decided me to try and overcome this antipathy.

My father and mother happened to be from home when I arrived, so I first of all spoke to the dispensary doctor, who resided in the village near us. He encouraged me to enter the profession, saying he would give me all the help he could. So I wrote to my father, telling him of my decision, and begging of him to apprentice me to my friend the doctor, reminding him that I was now sixteen and a half years old. My father readily consented to my becoming a doctor, but very wisely objected to my plan of education, and in a very short time all was settled to my satisfaction by my being apprenticed to Mr. Maurice Collis, at that time one of the surgeons attached to the Meath Hospital, Dublin. This was in June, 1844.

Apprenticeship at this time had ceased to be compulsory, but it was still not uncommon for medical students to be bound to leading surgeons, and to me it proved to be a great advantage. Mr. Collis was an old friend of my father's, and took a great interest in my welfare. After I was bound to him he advised my father to let me enter Trinity College, Dublin, with the view of enabling me to take the M.D. degree, as well as that in arts. My father agreed. I passed the entrance examination in July, 1844; and though my entering college entailed the double work of reading for the term examinations in classics, mathematics, etc., and studying medicine in all its branches, including anatomy, physiology, chemistry, etc., I undertook it readily. I never failed at any examination, though, as I have already said, I never had the advantage of private tuition in either medicine or classics. The aid of a "grinder" in medicine was so universal that for a man to obtain his diploma as a surgeon without the aid of one was most unusual.

CHAPTER V

DUBLIN
SEVENTY YEARS AGO

Improvement of Nassau Street—-Clearing the slums about St. Patrick's Cathedral—Sir Benjamin Guinness—Better houses—Dublin to Drogheda by rail—"Fly" boats on the canal—A wretched mode of travelling—The canal—Accidents and anecdotes—The 'bus in the canal—Strange method of raising it— I take to a tricycle and pitch head first into the canal — Dublin "Charleys"—Outside and inside cars—The fearsome "first" 'bus— The last sedan-chair—First gas Lights, bad and few—Changes—Social habits—The crinoline period

THE DUBLIN I knew in my childhood and youth was very different from the city of to-day. Many are the changes which have taken place during the seventy-two years which have elapsed since I, soon after the accession to the throne of Queen Victoria, first saw it. Great have been the improvements within its bounds, while the miles of suburbs now extending around it have been wholly built in my time.

Of improvements, I consider the widening of Nassau Street the greatest. In 1838 this street was hardly half its present width, and instead of the handsome railings which now separate it from the College Park, there ran a very high, very ugly, very dirty brick wall, so high that nothing could be seen over it but the sky, while the houses facing it were extremely mean. It was a narrow, dirty, shabby thoroughfare. Trinity College, I believe, not only gave the land needed for the widening of the street, but also contributed largely to the cost of the alterations.

Another great improvement effected in recent years, which, from a sanitary and philanthropic point of view, should be placed first, was the sweeping away of the filthy slums which surrounded St. Patrick's Cathedral, and the opening up of the approaches to it. This, and the erecting of a number of handsome artizans' dwellings, as well as the laying out of the grounds in front of the cathedral, is due to the liberality of Lord Iveagh. The cathedral had previously been restored by his father, the late Sir Benjamin Lee Guinness, at a cost of £150,000; while to Sir Benjamin's eldest son, Lord Ardilaun, the city is indebted for the handsome park known as St. Stephen's Green, which is a great ornament to the city. Before he took it in hand the park was nothing more than a large, ugly green space, from which the public were excluded, while inside the railings enclosing it no one was ever seen, except occasionally a nurse or two and some children, The park is nearly a mile in circumference.

But were a Rip Van Winkle now to awake after a seventy years' sleep, he would probably be most surprised at the changes which have taken place in the fine houses in the streets off Mountjoy and Rutland Squares, and in some of which he may have been a guest at ball or route—houses with lofty rooms, many of them having ceilings ornamented with beautiful stucco work. All these are now mere tenement houses, every room probably the home of a whole family. The class that formerly inhabited them have either, following fashion, migrated to the south side of the city, or occupied houses erected of recent years in the suburbs, tempted there by the facilities afforded by the tramways company, whose lines extend for miles beyond the confines of the city.

Then, in 1835, only one railway, the Dublin and Kingstown Railway, six miles long, existed in Ireland, and it was not till 1844 that the Dublin and Drogheda, thirty miles long, was opened, not to be completed to Belfast for many long years.

Travellers reached Dublin from the provinces in those days either by coach or by canal. On the latter plied "fly" boats, so-called on account of their speed (!), which reached five miles an hour when the locks were not numerous, and even six, it was boasted, on the long, level stretches.

This was a wretched mode of travelling. The boats were of course narrow. A table ran down the Centre of the cabin, with hard benches on either side of it for passengers to sit on, and if there were a good many travelling, you found when once seated, it was a difficult matter to move; so when travelling at night, as most people did, one sat without moving till morning. All this has long since become a thing of the past; Ireland, for its size and population, has as extended a railway system as England.

Speaking of canals, a sad accident of a most unusual kind happened, to my knowledge, in one of them. It was on a Sunday, I think about the year 1860, when I received an urgent summons to visit a lady residing in Rathmines, a suburb, the road to which crossed the canal by a low bridge, which was traversed at short intervals by omnibuses. At each side of the canal, where the parapet of the bridge ended, there was a wide opening leading to the bank of the canal, while directly under the bridge, but extending beyond it, was a lock, at that moment empty, the lower gate having been left open. At about 2 p.m. one of the 'buses approached the bridge at its usual slow pace; inside it were seven passengers, most of them ladies. All went well till, when near the top of the bridge, one of the horses became restive, and then began to back down the incline. The idea of danger seems never to have entered the driver's head. Back slowly went the 'bus, not straight, but gradually in a curve, down the roadway to the side of the lock, and then down into it, not sideways, but back end first, and so that it stood upright in the empty lock. The horses, of course, were dragged down too, and hung, plunging and kicking, suspended by the harness and still fastened to the pole. The coachman jumped off as the bus went down and rushed away, quite out of his mind. There were the poor passengers in the deep, dark, but nearly dry lock, unable to get out of the omnibus, while the horses kicked madly.

A crowd soon collected, but no one ventured to do anything, till some fool called out, "Shut the lower gate, fill the lock and the 'bus will float!" His suggestion was acted on with the natural result—as the water rose the seven wretched passengers were drowned, as also were the horses. It was to see an aunt of one of these unfortunate passengers I was called; her niece, a young, attractive woman, had only an hour or so previously left her house full of life.

Within a few hundred yards of the spot where this happened, I, a year after, got a man out of the canal who was near being drowned. Driving one day along a road close to its bank I heard "Help! help!" called out loudly, and saw a man in the very middle of the canal struggling vainly to reach the shore. I knew that, except in the very middle, the water was shallow. I jumped out of the carriage, unbuckled the reins, and in an instant threw him one end which he seized, and so I and my coachman succeeded in pulling him out. I did not wait to inquire how he got in, but whether by accident or on purpose, he got such a fright that I think he took care not to fall in again.

But my personal experiences of that part of the canal

were not yet over. When I was quite elderly, bicycles and tricycles began to come into vogue, and I got a tricycle, at first, mainly with the intention of being able to take exercise in the spring and summer months after my day's work was done; this usually was about five or six o'clock in the day. Naturally I chose the smoothest and quietest roads and that running along the side of the canal was such. One cold March afternoon I started for my first ride for the season, and was on this road when I reached a point where it was in very bad repair.

Between me and the canal ran the tow-path, which seemed nice and smooth, so I decided to get on it. To do this I had to cross a slight elevation where I fancy a bank once had been, separating the towing path from the road. I crossed this obliquely, but the incline towards the canal was sharper than I anticipated, and when my outside wheel reached the top of the rise, the machine overturned and I went head foremost into the water, the tricycle falling on the top of me. Of course I scrambled out in a minute, and pulled out the machine, but I had got a regular ducking, and must have presented a ridiculous figure. Imagine me, an old doctor of sixty, dripping from head to foot, for my head went in first, and in scrambling out, the water was up to my hips!

A man coming from one direction came offering help, while a respectable woman ran up quickly from the other, and with exclamations of pity, pulled out a small, clean pocket-handkerchief for me to dry myself with. The size of that article offered for the purpose seemed so ridiculous that I could not help laughing; however, it served to sop up the water off my face, and, as I shivered in the cold wind, I got up on my tricycle and rode home as hard as I could. A hot bath taken instantly on arrival warded off any subsequent trouble, but thereafter I gave the canal a wide berth on my rides.

My first visit to Dublin occurred Just before the old nightwatchmen—"Charleys" they were called—were abolished. They were a very useless, and, if all said of them be true, a very venal lot of old men. The stories told of the pranks played on them by the young bloods of the day were many. These incapable guardians were replaced by "the new police," and very soon a reformation in the state of the streets, especially at night, followed.

Then there were no cabs. The Irish "outside car," which still holds its own in Dublin, was in constant use. The old hackney coaches had given place to abominable vehicles known as the "inside car," used mainly by elderly ladies, but in wet weather by men too, and at night by ladies and gentlemen going to the theatre or to balls. They were most uncomfortable and hideously ugly.

Imagine a huge governess car, slung between a pair of very high wheels, surmounted by a body of wood with two little windows in front, the door, of course, behind, while the driver was perched up in front, his seat being nearly on a level with the top. The shafts were raised in front, to prevent the weight from resting on the horse's back; so much so that the passenger had of necessity to sit at the end of the car next the door, otherwise he would slip down to it.

It was a sight to see a portly old lady getting into one of these cars. The driver, of course, got down to open and shut the door, and his weight being removed from the front, up went the shafts high in the air and the fat passenger would be literally shoved up the incline and into the machine. When the driver had scrambled into his seat again equilibrium was somewhat restored, and then the jolting began. If you had luggage with you it had to be carried inside, and it danced about your legs as you jolted on. There were three or four passengers, those in front slipped down gradually on those in the rear.

Cabs were not introduced until about the year 1860 and came into use very slowly indeed, the inside car, in a modified form, and locally known as a "jingle," exists still in Cork.

The terms "inside" and "outside" cars puzzled strangers greatly, and a German gentleman one day asked a jarvey to explain the matter to him. This he did promptly, in these words, "Why, do ye see, the inside cars has their wheels outside, and outside cars their wheels inside of them!" a perfectly correct, if not very lucid explanation. I am able to state that this story is strictly true, though people thought it was invented by a clown who repeated it in a pantomime.

Omnibuses were not introduced into Dublin till about 1850, and then for a long time plied only on one route. So you had either to take an inside or outside car, or walk, and walk most of us did, and no doubt, were all the healthier for so doing. I had a standing invitation to go to dine whenever I liked with a family whose avenue gate was a little distance beyond the five-milestone from Dublin. I used to walk all the way there regularly once or twice a month and back again after 10 p.m., and thought nothing of it. Now, what with electric trams running in every direction (one takes you very near that house for threepence), and with the universal bicycle, walking seems doomed to become a lost art.

The introduction of the inside car put an end to the general use of sedan-chairs; for, notwithstanding the discomfort of the former, they were the handier and cheaper of the two. But in my student days sedan-chairs were not extinct, and occasionally you would see an elderly lady or some old swell borne in one of them by two men, sometimes in full livery, to a dinner party or dance; indeed, it is not so long since the last of these was removed from its stand at the corner of Hume Street, where it had rested unused for years.

The oil lamps with which the city had been previously lighted had given place to gas ere I knew Dublin, but gas lighting was in its infancy, and, as far as brilliancy was concerned, was no great improvement. The gas was bad, the lamp-posts far apart, and, though used for lighting the streets and public rooms, was rarely seen in private houses. There, wax candles were the correct thing, while amongst the poor dip-candles were the sole illuminant. In 1838 the streets of Dublin remained very dark, and were not quite safe at night. Now they are brilliant with electric light; and in this and many other things such a revolution has taken place since my childhood as the younger generation can hardly realise.

The changes in the social habits of the upper classes is hardly less marked than are those in respect to locomotion. There used to be promenades in the squares on every Sunday afternoon, those in Merrion Square being specially well attended and select, and during the summer months there were promenades on certain week-days also, when a band would play.

If you went to any of these you would be sure to meet many acquaintances, and I think their total cessation is a matter to be regretted. It was a pretty sight, too, to watch the well-dressed assemblage. The ladies' attire differed much from that now in vogue. Hats were unknown. Old and young alike wore bonnets, and very becoming they were. White stockings, too, were the fashion. Very anxious were the ladies that to soil or speck should mar them—no easy matter to avoid when walking the streets of "dear, dirty Dublin"—and often did I wonder how the girls managed to keep them so clean. Shoes with sandals were the correct thing.

Then came that hideous crinoline period, so well depicted in the pages of *Punch,* as ugly as inconvenient. If you got into a covered car or even a carriage with a lady, this affair had to be turned up like a huge screen, or no space would be left. One day I was walking with two young ladies when a man passed us with a piece of broken metal in his hand, it caught the dress of one of them and made a large angular rent in it, through which the wire hoops of her crinoline could be seen. How such accidents did not oftener happen, with dresses some five or more feet in diameter, is a wonder. As a rule, ladies disliked the fashion. Yet very few had courage to omit wearing the monstrosities. But are not the enormous hats now worn, even by quite old women, as absurd and as inconvenient as were the crinolines?

The dinner hour, too, has now become so much later that, as a result, luncheon has become an important meal; formerly a sandwich would suffice, or for young people perhaps bread-and-jam, while supper parties, which were then quite common, are now, except, indeed, at a restaurant after the play, things of the past. Their cessation is not to be regretted, for too often they ended in undue consumption of whiskey punch.

CHAPTER VI

OF THE BEGINNINGS OF
MANY THINGS

*Changes caused by the introduction of Steam locomotion—No annual
holidays—Occasional long visits to friends—I have no holiday tor twenty
five years—The price of postage prohibitive—Abuse of "franking" abolished
by penny post— Shocking railway carriages—A "fourth" class—Luggage
arrangements—Incidents on the rail—I am sent to the scene of an
accident—Potato famine stops enterprise—The strange story of a £20
note—Telegraphs —Evolution at the Irish newspaper— The Saunders'
Newsletter— Freeman's Journal—The Daily Express—Daniel O'Connell
and Lady Morgan—A remarkable blind beggar.*

If home life and social habits have changed greatly,
mainly by the decrees of fashion, even to a greater
degree have they been affected by the facilities for
movement afforded by the introduction of steam.
Especially affected by this is that great assemblage
comprised in the term "The Middle Classes," which
includes the families of professional men of all callings,
civil servants, and the many engaged in a multitude of
other avocations.

Seventy years ago the members of these families were
stay-at-homes. Travelling was tedious and expensive, and
the annual holiday, now universal, unknown. During the

long vacation, some of the members of the legal profession would stay away, but for the family or even a part of it to go off, as is now the case, was not thought of. A visit to relatives or friends, which meant a good long stay for the parents, accompanied by one or more grown-up daughters, was not uncommon; or a lodge or apartments might be taken every second or third year at a quiet seaside place, or some other attractive spot, not so far off that it could not be reached in a day's drive. Such a holiday, when it occurred, would be a matter talked of for a long time before, and furnished a theme for gossip subsequently.

The wealthy landowner occasionally built a "lodge," at a place where bathing could be indulged in during the summer, or shooting obtained in winter, to which the family and servants would migrate. But hotels such as are now to be seen everywhere did not exist. Doubtless there were many inns along the coach routes at which travellers stayed for a night, but no one thought of remaining at one of these unless detained by illness or business.

For myself, though I went from time to time during my early professional life to visit and spend a week or so at the house of some relatives, I never took such a holiday as is now understood by the term till I had been some twenty-five years in practice, and never a full month till I retired altogether. I quite approve of the hard-worked bread-winner having his holiday, but as a rule he needs rest, not perpetual travel, from which so many now annually return, weary in body and impoverished in purse.

Communication by letter was in my childhood as restricted as was travel, and very expensive. A letter from Dublin to our post town cost ninepence, and from most parts of England two-and-sixpence; indeed, on every letter I received from home during my first year at Maidstone the postage was two-and-ninepence, consequently those received or written were few and far between.

No doubt the system of "franking," a privilege enjoyed by peers and members of parliament, mitigated in a trifling degree the severity of the impost, at least, to those who could get a member to frank a letter for him, which was done by his affixing his signature in the left-hand comer of the letter. This privilege was greatly abused. Some members affixed their signature to any number of letters, although they were restricted to two a day; but, provided they were posted in different post offices and addressed to different localities, detection was impossible. This system was put an end to when the penny postage came in.

The carriages for railways were built at first exactly on the pattern of the old coaches, and it looked as if the bodies of three or four of them had been bolted together and put on a truck. The luggage, too, was placed on the roof and covered with a tarpaulin strapped down, just as in the old coaching days; while, to complete the resemblance, the guard was perched on the top of a carriage with his feet on a footboard. Of course there were, I presume no tunnels and few bridges to pass under on the lines on which I saw this arrangement, and the speed of the trains seldom exceeded twenty miles an hour.

As to the luggage, the plan of carrying it on the top of the carriage you travelled in did well enough if you were to arrive at a terminus, but to get luggage down at a roadside station involved much trouble and delay. The third-class carriages were merely wooden boxes, open on the sides, placed on trucks; on some lines there was a fourth class, consisting of trucks pure and simple, with a bench running round the sides. These benches were quickly occupied, and later passengers had to stand. I travelled in one of these so-called carriages in Yorkshire once, but at the second stoppage had to leave it and get into a second-class one. Their use was interdicted ere long.

Then, if an engine broke down, electric telegraphy being unknown, the passengers had to wait till the next train came up. On two occasions the engines drawing the train I was in broke down at about 8 or 9 p.m. On the first occasion I spent the night till 5 a.m. at a wretched little roadside station, without a fire, and without the possibility of getting as much as a cup of tea. On the second, we had to remain in the train, as we were not near a station, till about the same hour in the morning, when the night mail train came up and brought us on. On that occasion a fellow passenger who was coming up to attend a grand fancy-dress ball, arrived just in time to see the last of the tired-out, dilapidated-looking waiters walking out of the public rooms in which it had been held.

But far worse was the result of a similar breakdown of an engine, in broad daylight, which occurred near Sallins Station some sixteen miles from Dublin about this time. It was being followed by a heavy goods train, the driver of which seems not to have kept a good look-out. Anyway, his train dashed into the standing one, nine passengers, I think, being killed and many injured. On hearing of the accident I, then a young man, was sent down by the insurance company to render aid, and I shall never forget the sight of the bodies of those ladies and gentlemen lying side by side in a shed close to the station. One gentleman's head had been cut off as by an axe.

The terrible poverty which overwhelmed Ireland as the result of the potato famine put a stop for a time to railway enterprise in that country, and great inconvenience was caused by the long delay in completing even the main lines. There was no money in the country. English capitalists had little confidence in the future of any Irish undertaking, and the Government, while sanctioning lavish expenditure of money on useless roads in out-of-the-way districts, would not advance any to be expended on the opening up of the country by the making of railways, or even towards completing the main lines, all which have since proved financial successes.

Thus years elapsed before the line between Dublin and Belfast was complete. There was a gap of over fifty miles between Drogheda and Portadown, where the line from Belfast stopped. This gap had to be traversed—if at night, by mail coach; if by day, on along, two-horse car, which, if it had springs at all, nevertheless jolted one so horribly that their existence could hardly be deemed possible. As a consequence of this break an acquaintance of mine had a curious experience with a £20 banknote. Travelling to Dublin from Belfast, he had changed to the mail coach at Portadown and by it reached Drogheda somewhere about 4 a.m. There he purchased a ticket to Dublin, handing in what he thought was a £1 note and receiving from the clerk the correct change as if it had been such. Next morning he discovered on examining his pocket-book that the £20 note was gone. Obviously he must have handed it by mistake to the clerk, for he had no money with him except the two notes, and that for £1 was safe in his pocket-book.

Telegrams being unknown, he had no resource hut to go to the Dublin terminus and tell his story, to be informed that as the clerk at Drogheda had sent in all money received by him up to 9 a.m., and as his accounts were perfectly correct, they feared the £20 note had not come into his hand; but that they would make inquiries and directed him to call the next day. On his doing so, he was rejoiced to have his money handed him. It had been brought to the office by a gentleman, late the day before. He, too, had travelled from Belfast by the mail on the preceding night, and had handed the booking clerk a £5 note saying that he had none for a smaller amount, and had received as change what he assumed to be four £1 notes and some silver, all of which he put into his pocket without examining, as he was in a hurry to secure his seat, there being a good many passengers clamouring for tickets.

On arriving at his hotel he went to bed, and did not get up till near midday; then, having dressed and lunched, he went and voted at the election for a member of parliament for the University then being held. Later in the day he proceeded to do some business in the town, one matter being to pay a bill for a small amount due to his bootmaker, and for this purpose handed him what he supposed to be a £1 note. The man looked at it, said he was sorry he had not change for a note of that amount, and that the banks had closed. The gentleman could not at first understand what was the difficulty, as he only expected a shilling or so of change, and some minutes elapsed ere he realised that he had received £28 in exchange for his £5 note. Then, seeing that he must have got the note from the clerk at Drogheda, betook it at once to the head office. Thus a £20 note passed through three hands before its value was realised by the fourth to whom it was presented. All the parties were pleased at the result. The loser was glad to get back a sum of money he could ill spare, and the finder to be able to clear the clerk from any possible suspicion of dishonesty which might have rested on him had not the note been traced.

Hardly second in importance to the introduction of steam as a means of locomotion on sea and land has been the harnessing of electricity, which in my youth was only known as a phenomenon to be exhibited at some scientific lecture. The electric telegraph, so far as our planet is concerned, has virtually annihilated time and space; while electricity as a motive power already threatens the supremacy of steam, though what it is remains unknown. Man's intellect has failed to discover this. It may be that the human mind has in this direction come to its limit. The fiat may have gone forth, "So far shalt thou go and no farther"; but whether this be so or not, certain it is that the uses of electricity will in the near future be largely extended, but to what extent it is impossible even to guess.

Little less wonderful has been the marvellous evolution of the newspaper and the extension of the influence of the press which has taken place within the last fifty years. In my student days there was, to the best of my belief, but one daily paper published in Ireland— *The Saunders' Newsletter,* "price fourpence." It was what was called a "scissors paper," the contents, of course excluding advertisements, being made up nearly altogether of matter copied from English papers and which nowadays would be considered quite stale. News published in London or Manchester on a Monday would not as a rule appear until Thursday.

I have by me a copy of this paper of June 19, 1824 (that, of course, was before I was born). In it is published the summary of the proceedings of parliament on June 15. This copy consists of one sheet of four pages; each page is twenty inches long by thirteen in width, and contains four columns. Of the sixteen columns in -the whole paper, not quite six are devoted to "news," and under that term are included two devoted to parliamentary proceedings. Of the two remaining columns, more than half of one is taken up with the account of the search for the body of a poor malformed child which had been exhibited as a wonder under the title of "The Sicilian Dwarf," though it had been born in Ireland.

The rest of the paper is taken up with advertisements greatly spaced out, amongst them one announcing the sale by the Customs of 517,000 lb. of "seized and legally condemned tobacco." The paper also contains an advertisement stating that a charity sermon would be preached on the ensuing Sunday, in St. George Church, Dublin, by the Rev. Wm. Atthill (my father). This paper was given to me by an old patient who remembered him. The paper had no leading article of any description; and as to politics it was colourless—and so continued till its demise some forty years ago.

As far as I know this was the only daily paper in my

early days. The *Freeman's Journal* which, though established as early as 1763, did not become such till it came into the possession of the late Sir John Grey. Sir John was a man of great ability, and it is mainly owing to his exertions, and to the influence which his paper had gained, that the citizens of Dublin are indebted for the ample supply of pure soft water it now possesses. The Act authorizing the formation of the Vartry reservoir was obtained in 1861.

As the price of *Saunders' Newsletter* was quite above its value, and as fourpence a copy was a heavy tax on persons of limited means, there was a regular trade established for the lending of it at a penny per hour. One person got it, say, at eight o'clock; it would be called for at nine o'clock, when his neighbour had it, and so on; or you could buy one of these copies in the afternoon for twopence, and then, as they were all impressed with a Government stamp, you could forward it to a friend postage free.

About 1853 *The Daily Express* was established. It had leading articles and a strong political bias; and, as it was double the size of *Saunders'*, at once became a formidable competitor. It, too, used to be lent out for an hour, and its proprietors organised a system which enabled travellers on the Dublin and Kingstown line of railway to have a read for a penny while travelling. You could buy a copy for fourpence at either terminus, but the man at the other end would take it back from you, giving you threepence; the journey occupied half an hour. This system must have paid well. It was from a copy thus taken by me to read in the train that I first learned of the death of my old schoolfellow, Major Baldwin, already alluded to. *Saunders'* gradually sank and died out under the competition which ensued on the repeal of the duty on paper, the Act requiring every copy to be stamped before being issued. It had a very long and, from a commercial point of view, successful career. In my youth a weekly paper sufficed for the great majority of the country gentlemen.

Dan O'Connell, as he was universally called, and who occupied such a large space in the history of Irish politics, was still much before the public while I was a student. I well remember seeing him walking down Sackville Street with his cloak wrapped about him, a large, burly man; but his health was breaking down, and it was this reason that made him begin to wear the cloak. In his statue on the monument erected to his memory in Sackville Street he is portrayed as wearing the cloak. Many of his friends objected to this, as it represents him in the period of his decline. I remember Sir Dominic Corrigan expressing himself very strongly on this point; indeed, I think he resigned his seat on the committee entrusted with the task of erecting the statue in consequence; certainly he told me he would do so.

Speaking of O'Connell reminds me of Lady Morgan, a contemporary of his, who, though no longer living in

Dublin, was often spoken of. She was a remarkable woman, an authoress, a great conversationalist, and for years a prominent personage in Irish society. While young she attracted the attention of Lady Abercorn, who took her into her household, where she met Dr. Morgan, a man much her senior, whom she finally and rather reluctantly married. The marriage proved a happy one. Lady Abercorn induced the Lord Lieutenant to confer knighthood on the doctor, and they settled in Dublin. Her name, coupled with O'Connell's, was introduced into a ballad I used often to hear quoted. It ran thus:—

> "O Dublin, dear, there is no doubting,
> Beats every city upon the sea,
> For there you'll hear O'Connell spouting
> And Lady Morgan drinking tea,
> For 'tis the capital of the greatest nation,
> With the finest pisintry on fruitful sod
> Fighting like—— for conciliation
> And murdering each other for the love of God."

I quote from memory as I heard it repeated. I never saw the verse in print.

A remarkable character, but of a very different class, passed away about the time I entered college, namely, Zozimus, the blind beggar. This man would post himself in a quiet corner off a busy thoroughfare or, indeed, sometimes in a much-frequented street, and would quickly be surrounded by a crowd, listening to his witty remarks or to his replies to questions put to him by bystanders who invariably got the worst of it; or, more frequently, listening while he recited a ballad—it might be an impromptu, but more often one composed by himself previously. I recollect one of these in doggerell verse, descriptive of the finding of Moses amongst the bulrushes. After alluding to the decree ordering the destruction of all male Hebrew infants, he described Pharaoh's daughter as "Walking along the banks of the Nile" and preparing to bathe. Then came a couple of lines I still remember:—

> "She jumped into the water to wash her skin,
> Coming out she kicked the basket the child lay in,"—

and so on.

But in truth neither his witty replies nor ballads were calculated to improve the morals of his hearers, though nothing absolutely improper was ever uttered by him. Often he was very amusing, as when on one occasion a lot of street Arabs were pestering him, he suddenly stopped in the middle of his recitation and, sweeping his stick angrily all round him, exclaimed: —

" Begone, ye's blackguards! I know ye's well, Far better than the tongue can tell."

He received a good deal of money, and his fame is not, even yet, extinct in Dublin.

CHAPTER VII

SUNSHINE AND CLOUDS

Life of a medical student—Bleeding still practised—Operations before anaesthetics—The happiest year of my life was 1846—My brother and I go yachting—A memorable night—The yacht is crippled —My home life ends—Home memories.

THE LIFE of a medical student has not varied materially since I was one, sixty-five years ago. Then, as now, there were the steady and industrious, the idle and the dissipated; but as to the length of time to be devoted to the study of medicine, in the methods of teaching and in the subjects to be taught, there has been a vast change. At that time a surgical diploma might be, and as in my own case was, obtained in three years; now five years' study is compulsory. The subjects to be studied have increased in number, and the methods of teaching altered; but these changes, great and important as they are, are little in comparison with the revolution which has taken place in the practice of both medicine and surgery during the last fifty years.

Everyone has read or heard of the practice, in bygone days, of bleeding patients from a vein in the arm for every form of real or imaginary disease. This practice, though on the wane when I became a student, had not been wholly given up. I was taught to bleed before I was an apprentice a month. But apart from this, the revolution which has taken place in other respects in my days are so great as probably to seem incredible, at least to the younger portion of the present generation.

Now, if an operation has to be performed, the patient inhales an anaesthetic—frequently as he or she lies in bed, is removed while unconscious to the operating theatre, and after a time awakes to find himself still in bed, but to be told that the dreaded operation is "all over."

Formerly the patient would most probably have walked to the operation room, would have been terrified by seeing the needful preparations made, and been in an agony of fear at the thought of the sufferings to be endured. Assistants would be standing by to hold him down in case he struggled, and often the patient had to be strapped down. A few, but only a few, bore heroically the pain. which must be inflicted by even the most skilful surgeon; and the groans, cries and struggles of the many were most distressing to hear and see. Now all is done in perfect stillness; there is no need to hurry, as there is no pain to be borne. Formerly the mortality after operations was very great, even in favourable cases. Now a fatal termination is comparatively rare, and in favourable cases virtually never occurs. Formerly the rounds inflicted by the surgeon required weeks, indeed, not infrequently months, to heal. Now it is generally a matter of merely a few days. All this is due to the use of the antiseptic methods introduced by Lord Lister, to whom the whole world owes a debt of gratitude which neither money nor the title so worthily bestowed could repay. To-day thousands of sufferers are annually restored to health who, less than fifty -years ago, would certainly have died.

Looking back on the years long passed, 1845, the second year of my apprenticeship, seems to me the happiest year in my whole life. I was greatly interested in my professional studies, especially so in hospital work. I had pleased my father by my application and steadiness, and as, to my inexperienced eyes, his health seemed fairly good, there was nothing to mar the summer vacation, the last I ever spent in the dear home of my childhood. My eldest brother, then a widower, was over on a visit, and he aided us in buying a small yacht, in which we sailed over the waters of lovely Lough Erne, which afforded me the greatest possible pleasure. We would land on one of the numerous islands in the lough, light a fire, and have what seemed to me a delicious picnic. The lunch would be composed, however, of only the plainest materials, of which the invariable potful of boiled potatoes formed a prominent part. But how we ever escaped being drowned I know not. We kept no sailor, and none of us really understood the management of a sail, though an elder brother who sometimes accompanied us thought he did; and that lake is a treacherous and dangerous one, squalls coming down suddenly from the hills. Often, too, it was very rough, so much so that I have been seasick on it. But of that we took but little heed.

On one never-to-be-forgotten night we were becalmed miles from home, and had to spend the night on a small, uninhabited island on which we landed after dark, the boat being anchored close inshore. We speedily lighted a fire, made a hearty meal of such food as remained to us, and slept soundly under the trees, with a blanket, which just covered the four of us, as a protection from the heavy dew. The yacht was too small to admit of our sleeping on board.

But more vivid still is the recollection of the last sail I ever had on that lake. One day, late in the autumn, I and a brother somewhat older than myself, decided to go out alone. When we reached the shore we found it was blowing so hard that my brother was against our starting; but I overcame his reluctance, and away we went, steering for an island some four miles off, and though it was blowing hard we almost reached it. But to get into shelter and to a safe anchorage we had to tack to clear a point lying outside our intended landing place. In doing this, our little boat missed stays in the heavy sea which was running on the point, and was driven on to the rocks. My brother could not swim; I could, so instantly stripping off my coat I jumped out to find myself in shallow water. We quickly lowered our sails and endeavoured with poles to get off again, but our strength was insufficient for the task. Fortunately help soon came, for the farmer who lived on the island saw us, and he and his man ran down to our aid, and with their help we succeeded in getting our little yacht into a sheltered anchorage; but her rudder was smashed, and other damage done which rendered returning in her impossible.

The hospitable farmer brought us to his cottage, where his wife boiled potatoes for us and dried our clothes. Then he took us in his boat and landed us on a large island about half a mile off. This island was nearly three miles long, its length running parallel to the shore of the mainland, and we knew that at its extreme end we would be able to get a boat to put us ashore, the channel there being narrow.

But we had to walk more than two miles to reach that point, and after that four more to tramp to our home, and it was getting late.

I had on a pair of old shoes which had been re-soled. These had become soaked, for I had been standing in water up to my waist for a long time while trying to save the boat; and during our long tramp down the island the soles loosened, and I had to pull the loose soles off, and walk the rest of the way as best I could. We got home long after dark, wet, weary, and very hungry, but quite cheery.

But our crippled yacht had to be got to her moorings preparatory to hauling her up for the winter, during which she would be repaired. To accomplish this it was necessary to get the loan of a large boat belonging to a friend, and tow her home. We decided to do this the very next day if fine. Now, I used, during vacation, to help our doctor, on each of his dispensary days, to make up medicine for the poor; and as the day following our adventure was one of these, my brother agreed to meet me at twelve o'clock. We would then go on and get the boat back. He was to bring our lunch with him. But twelve o'clock, came and he did not appear, so on I went alone, supposing he would overtake me, which he never did. He said afterwards that he considered it was too stormy. I arrived at the spot where my friend's boat lay, and got on board her, with his two sailors. We soon reached our derelict yacht, and were quickly under way, having her in tow. Then I began to feel the pangs of hunger, for I had tasted nothing since an eight o'clock breakfast. But there was nothing for me to eat! the sailors had dined in their cottages before I arrived, and there was not a scrap of food in the boat.

Our little yacht was fitted with lockers, and it occurred to me there might be something in them that could be eaten. So, hauling her close up to us, I scrambled on board to find them locked and I without keys. I soon forced the lock, to discover just one apple much decayed, about a couple of square inches of very dry cheese and a scraping of jam in the bottom of a pot—not a sumptuous lunch for a very hungry lad of seventeen, but I spread the jam on the cheese, and finished with all that was eatable of the apple, and felt better.

That ended not only my yachting season, but virtually

my home life. I went up to Dublin a few weeks later, and I only returned in the following summer for a short stay. Then, my father's health compelling him to seek further medical advice, I left home with him, never to return, for he died at his son's house the following spring, and the glebe house passed into the hands of a stranger.

What is it that attaches us all, poor and rich alike, to the home of our childhood and infancy? Mine had little really attractive about it—a plain, square, two-story parsonage, standing on the side of a hill which had been bare till a few years before my birth, when plantations had been laid out round it by my father. The view on either side was bounded by hills still barer and higher, separated from us by only a couple of fields. But from the front the lake could be seen distinctly just two miles off. We had no near neighbours.

I had no boys of my own age to play with. Yet I loved the place, and when seriously ill of typhoid fever forty years ago, I invariably, on rousing from my restless, troubled sleep, had the gate lodge, with the large beech tree which grew beside it, pictured, as it were, before my eyes. I can realise what the poet Cowper's feelings must have been when he wrote that beautiful poem in memory of his mother.

CHAPTER VIII

THE POTATO FAMINE

*Potato blight appears in 1846—Conditions of people in 1847 "awful" —
Potatoes almost the only food of the people—Easy way of getting married—
Also an easy path to poverty—Runaway matches—Rotting potatoes—Stench
from the fields—The starving people—Plenty of money but no food—Waste
of money on useless "relief works"—Maize meal adds to the misery and
death rate—Its preparation not understood—Derelict "relief works"—I
become a full blown surgeon.*

The potato blight, as it was called, manifested itself in the summer of 1846, and during the succeeding winter the great scarcity of food pressed with daily increasing severity on the poor, while in 1847 the condition of matters in Ireland became awful.

For many years previously the great mass of the rural population had lived solely on potatoes. Early marriages were the rule, and it was quite common for lads of eighteen or twenty to marry, settling down in a cabin built of sods, and living a life little above that of a pig—which animal, indeed, was often the joint occupier of the cabin, if the price of a young one could by any means be scraped together. This was the era when the morality of the Irish peasant was so conspicuous.

There was in those days an easy way of getting married if parents objected. The boy and girl would "run away" together some evening after dark to a neighbour's house, where they would be almost invariably received. The news would gradually spread of what had occurred, the neighbours would flock in, and whiskey would soon be forthcoming, for many of those who came would bring some with them, and the night would be spent in singing songs and general gaiety. The "runaway" pair always sat up the whole night through with the company.

In the morning the lad would return to his father's house, but the girl remained behind. The pair saw little of each other till the wedding took place, which it always did with the least possible delay; for the girl would never be permitted to re-enter her parents' house till she was married.

I knew of many of these runaway matches, and in 1846, our housemaid having gone off thus one evening with a lad who worked for my father, I and my brother went to the house where they were, and stayed some time to see what was going on.

No wonder, then, that Ireland was over-populated, or that it had eight million inhabitants within its narrow limits, two-thirds of whom lived nearly wholly on potatoes!

Well do I remember the beginning of the catastrophe which depopulated Ireland, and for a time paralyzed the country. As early as May, 1846, attention was called to the disease, which, appearing first amongst potatoes planted in rich land on which they had been grown for years without intermission, soon spread in all directions. As the summer advanced, not a district in the whole island but was affected.'

My father, being obliged to go to Dublin to obtain medical advice, and being unable to bear the jolting of a stage coach or the fatigue of such a journey, travelled in a carriage by easy stages, staying for a day or two at the houses of friends *en route* till we reached Drogheda, from whence the railway was open to Dublin.

I travelled with him, and, sitting on the box seat with the coachman, and thus having an extended view, soon began to realise as I had not done previously, what just grounds there were for the universal alarm which existed.

Driving, say, for half a mile or more through smiling meadow or pasture lands, you would suddenly perceive an offensive stench, borne on the wind; then into view would come a field, often of large size, one mass of blackened stalks, a clear indication that the tubers were already rotting.

But no one yet realised the full extent of the awful calamity which had befallen the country. The old crop lasted yet a while, and for a time oatmeal could be had, though at enhanced prices. And it was not till the new year (1847) had fairly set in that the cry came from every quarter that "the people were starving."

Then money was freely given, coming mainly from England, and was also voted by parliament, to be expended on relief works. But the great difficulty was to bring food to the starving people; indeed, it was almost impossible to convey it in sufficient quantities to those living in remote districts along the West coast of Ireland, where the people were dying daily by hundreds. There were virtually no railways in Ireland then, and the food stuffs had to be carted from the sea-ports and through districts often without roads; and when it did reach these poor, famished people, it was mainly in the form of the then, to them, unknown Indian meal—an excellent food, but requiring to be thoroughly cooked to be digestible. This they did not realise, and it was largely consumed when not half boiled, and, sad to say, instead of nourishing the people, actually increased the mortality, inducing, as it did, bowel complaints that soon proved fatal.

The relief works, too, when started, were for the most part not only of a useless nature, but very badly managed. There was no proper organisation and little, if, indeed any, supervision. A batch of men would be started, say, to cut down a hill on some out-of-the-way road: they dawdled, worked in fits and starts, and in the cold, wet weather got chilled, and died by the score. Then roads were laid out, and never finished; and, in truth, most of these would have been, if finished, absolutely useless.

Throughout the whole of Ireland the same system existed, and when, several years later, the relief works were closed, there was not a county in Ireland in which many roads were not left in an almost impassable state— hills half cut down, hollows partially filled, nothing completed. What between want, waste, ignorance, incapacity and mismanagement vast sums of money were uselessly expended, and thousands of lives lost which might have been saved. For twenty years after the famine many roads in all parts of Ireland remained in the conditions I have described, and not a few remain so to the present day, while new ones laid out remain derelict. I speak of what I have seen myself, not from hearsay.

One man in his place in parliament urged that the money voted be expended in building trunk lines of railway, which were greatly needed, but the Government of the day turned a deaf ear to his entreaties. Lord George Bentinck spoke in vain, and this great opportunity of benefiting the country permanently was lost; moreover, had the money voted been so expended, it would have proved a remunerative investment, and the Irish railways would now be the property of the nation.

I was resident in Dublin during the first two years of the famine, for but little more than half of the five years for which I had been bound were expired when my father died, and his income dying with him I feared that means might be wanting to admit of my serving out my time.

Therefore, as soon as I had completed the three years' curriculum of lectures and hospital attendance required by the College of Surgeons from candidates for their diploma, I explained to Mr. Collis my position, and begged time to sanction my presenting myself for examination. This he reluctantly did, and passing it, I found myself a full-blown surgeon when only nineteen years and a half old. This was in July, 1847. Fortunately, I was enabled to remain in Dublin for another year, and then tried to complete my university course.

CHAPTER IX

I BEGIN TO PRACTISE

A qualified surgeon—Appointed to the Fleet Street Dispensary—Appalling condition of sick poor of Dublin—Tenement houses—The voice from the far corner—I wish to remove to a hunting country as dispensary doctor—I withdraw and am not elected—A strange request—Surgeon to the Geashill Dispensary—Primitive arrangements—My lodgings in the thatched cottage—Famine distress still continues—Food very scarce—Population diminished through death and emigration—I am as poor as my neighbours—I move to Dublin In 1850.

BEING NOW a qualified surgeon, I succeeded in obtaining during the winter of 1847-48, an appointment on the staff of a charitable institution, known as the Fleet Street Dispensary, established with the view of affording medical attendance to the sick poor, who, were visited at their homes as well as prescribed for at the institution. None of the staff received any remuneration; on the contrary, we were required to obtain two subscribers of one guinea each or pay these subscriptions out of our own pockets! I gladly accepted the appointment on these terms, for I hoped to gain some experience thereby.

The condition of the sick poor in Dublin was at this date and for many years subsequently truly appalling.

The famine, due to the failure of the potato crop, had lasted for a year and a half. In all parts of the country there was the greatest distress, and in remote districts absolute starvation; hundreds died of starvation, thousands of "famine fever," as it was termed, typhoid not having been recognised or known, while typhus in its worst form was epidemic. Whole districts were depopulated by famine and fever, thousands emigrated to America, while the towns and cities were crowded by hosts of starving men, women and children, who thronged the streets begging for food. Some sought employment which could not be obtained, while hospitals and poor-houses were filled to excess. Temporary hospitals, known as the "fever sheds," were erected outside the city, but even these failed to supply sufficient accommodation for the famine-stricken multitude of sick. What the work of the dispensary doctor who laboured amongst this poverty-stricken mass of humanity was like, when overtaken by disease, may be imagined, but can hardly be described.

The tenement houses in which the poor lived were crowded from attic to cellar. I have known four families, each consisting of several individuals, living in one small room, a corner allotted to each family, without a stick of furniture amongst them. One instance I never shall forget. I narrate it to give some idea of the hopelessness of the task devolving on the medical man at this sad period.

My district embraced the low-lying slums contiguous to the river Liffey. One day I received a ticket directing me to visit a woman in one of these streets, not of the worst class. Calling at the address given, I was told that the patient lived in the "kitchen," and as there was no communication between the house proper and the so-called kitchen I had to go out of the front door and down into the area to gain entrance. There I found the woman in a veritable cellar, into which neither air nor light could enter, save through the door. Her case was one of typhus fever, so I gave her an order for admission to the fever hospital.

Before leaving I was asked to see another patient in the "back room," which I did. As it was pitch dark there, they lit a candle. Both these rooms were below the high-water mark of the river, which was but a few yards distant. The outer cellar was bad enough, but the back one was frightful. There was neither window nor fireplace in it. The walls, which were wholly below the level of the ground, had never been plastered; down them trickled little streams of water, the floor was saturated with damp, the air foul, while on a kind of bed raised a few inches from the floor lay a girl ill with small-pox. It is not a matter of surprise that the lives of several of the doctors engaged in this practice were lost from diseases contracted in these wretched dens.

On another occasion I was sent to visit a woman

residing in a lane, the house having no basement. It was late on a winter day, and twilight. Arrived at the house I pushed the outer door in, and knocked on that of the first room I came to. Hearing no answer, I opened it and asked, "Is there anyone here?" The room was pitch dark. I could see nothing, but a voice from the far corner said, "Yes." Asking was she Mrs. ——, "Yes," again came the reply. So I crept cautiously in the direction from whence the voice came. I could not see the patient, but, stooping down, felt the outline of a human form stretched on a little straw in the corner. There was no fire, no candle in the room, and as far as I could judge not a scrap of furniture. I asked her to raise her hand, and I felt the pulse; it was that of fever. I told her to put out her tongue, and, touching it, felt it as dry as a coarse file. I knew that it must be a case of typhus—alone, friendless, untended, without light, without fire, without food. Such was the daily experience of the physician. The only chance was to get such removed quickly to the "fever sheds," erected outside the city, for the hospitals in the city were filled to excess.

No wonder the mortality was great not amongst the poor patients only, but also amongst the medical men who attended them for not a few contracted the deadly disease and laid down their lives in the discharge of their duty.

The institution to which I was attached was very badly managed, and its funds quite insufficient for the purposes for which it had been established. However, I continued to work in it for a year; then, it being impossible for me to remain in Dublin holding a post to which no income was attached, I determined to become a candidate for an appointment in the country, which had become vacant through the death of the doctor from fever. The place was situated in a nice district some fifty miles from Dublin, a hunting country, with many gentry resident in the neighbourhood. Amongst them were relations of my mother; so I thought I had a good chance of success, and, indeed, at first, so did my friends who very kindly brought me forward. But fate, or rather, as I now believe, the guiding hand of God, interposed.

A lady, the daughter of a gentleman of influence amongst the electors, brought about my defeat, she believing, it was said, that the deceased doctor intended to marry her, though they were not engaged. She mourned for him somewhat loudly, and a distant relative of his, quite an old man, becoming a candidate, she induced her father to use his influence in his behalf, though previously he had been altogether in my favour. Then a certain number of the electors very fairly objected to my youth; I lacked a few days of being twenty-one, and the lady's friends urged this very strongly against me. My friends, seeing that, if these two sections united, they would not only fail to secure my election, but would find themselves saddled with a very elderly and, as they believed, incompetent medical man, hesitated. I knew nothing of this until the day before the election, when I was told it on my arrival at the house of a friend, a warm supporter of mine. He explained to me the position of matters, and asked me would I consent to withdraw if, on the following day, my supporters saw that they could not secure my election. Of course, though greatly disappointed, I gave my consent, with the result that a third man, whom no one particularly wished for, obtained the post.

Some twenty-five years after this, when I had become well known, a sister of the above lady wrote to me asking me to admit into the hospital of which I was the head a servant of hers. I recognised at once who the writer was, and in sending the order for admission reminded her that her father had prevented my election as their dispensary doctor in bygone days. To this she replied that his having done so was the best thing that could have happened to me, and so I believe it to have been. My failure to obtain that appointment influenced my whole future career. Had I obtained it, I most probably should have spent my whole life there, or at best have moved after a few years to some of the small towns in the neighbourhood where I might perhaps have had a somewhat larger, but still unimportant sphere for practice. As it was, within a couple of months I was elected surgeon to the Geashill Dispensary district in King's County, which was situated in such a poor and uninviting district that no medical man would remain there a day longer than he could help;

so when a chance of moving to Dublin occurred I at once availed myself of it, a move which I am satisfied I would not have made had I been settled in a pleasant locality, for at that time I never thought of moving to Dublin or that I could ever succeed there.

The village of Geashill in which I settled down on January 1, 1849, is situated midway between the towns of Portarlington and Tullamore, in an oasis in the midst of an immense tract of country covered with peat, and known as the Bog of Allen, and which occupies such a large space in the centre of Ireland. It was a very poor, but, for Ireland, a clean little place. The village was triangular in form. From the apex there ran on your left hand, as you entered coming from Portarlington, a long row of thatched, one-storied cottages. The first of these was the village shop, while at the other end stood a two-storied, slated house, in which the dispensary was held. In front of this row ran a stream of water, which would have been clear and bright but for the constant presence of numerous ducks and geese which were always paddling in it. The base of the little village was formed by a shorter row of rather better houses, some of them slated. On the third side stood the church, with graveyard attached, inclosed by a pretty high wall. The centre of the triangle thus formed was grassy, and was used as a fair green. Close to the church, and a little back from the road, stood the mansion of the lord of the manor, if I may use that expression. His lordship resided in England and it was not then inhabited, save by a caretaker.

No medical man had ever resided there previously, the dispensary having been served by a doctor living six miles off. As there was no house for me to live in, I had to put up with lodgings in the only place in the village where such could be obtained. This was a long, low, one-storied, thatched cottage, already mentioned. There were in it just four rooms, all mud-floored. The kitchen, in the centre, was the family day room (they slept in a windowless loft over it, reached by a ladder, which I was never permitted to ascend). Off the kitchen to the right was a small room in which were for sale a limited supply of groceries and unlimited supply of whiskey. Opening off the kitchen to the left was my sitting-room, with a hard, dry, earth floor, the centre covered with matting. It was a fair-sized room, about 15 or 16 ft. square. Off it was my bedroom which was only 7 ft by 15 ft. Its floor, also of earth, became, in wet weather, very damp and soft. To enter or leave my apartments I had to go through the kitchen, which, on market days, was thronged with customers. Sometimes a customer would open my door and look in, but I was always treated with great respect and courtesy, and I spent the winter months from January 1, 1849, very contentedly there, poor though the place was. I had plenty to do amongst the poor, and I had to read for my M.D. degree, for which I passed the examination early in the spring.

Later on I moved into a house some little distance from the village.

The country at this time was suffering, though with lessening severity, from the effects of the famine, which had lasted for more than two years; actual starvation hardly occurred now, for large quantities of Indian meal had been imported, and could be obtained at a low price, or was distributed gratuitously to the very poor; but there was great want of proper food everywhere.

It was useless to plant potatoes, for the blight was sure to show itself, and was rarely attempted except by those who could afford to import seed, and to plant it in carefully selected ground, but even so the crop often would become diseased. The population had been greatly diminished by the enormous emigration, as well as by the terrible mortality, due to famine and fever, though food was seldom absolutely wanting. Everywhere, even in King's County only fifty miles from Dublin, it was so difficult to obtain food in sufficient quantities that I knew of families being reduced to the necessity of eating boiled nettles to eke out their scanty meals.

But it was more from the want of money than from the absence of food that farmers suffered; there seemed to be absolutely no money in the country districts. Of course, this seriously affected medical men. For, myself, my salary was but £80 a year, and as my district was large, and as I had two dispensaries to attend some miles apart,

I had to keep a horse. Need I say I was nearly as poor as any of my neighbours? No doubt I did get what private practice the district afforded, but as there were only about three or four families in it who could pay a doctor anything, my income from that source was very small. This was the state of things when, most unexpectedly, came the offer of a post in Dublin, one which would produce an income about equal to my salary in the Country. I accepted it, though with some hesitation, and moved up to Dublin in September, 1850, after a residence in Geashill of somewhat less than two years.

I was sorry for some reasons to leave a place where the few gentry in the neighbourhood had shown me much kindness. With the poor I had been on the most friendly terms, and I think I had gained their confidence as a doctor to an extent I was hardly entitled to, for I had learned one thing from being thrown entirely on my own resources in an isolated district, at an immature age, and with so little experience; this was that I was painfully deficient in the knowledge of my profession. Had it not been for this, and for my desire to improve myself, I do not think I should have attempted to start in practice in the city.

CHAPTER X

QUEEN VICTORIA
VISITS DUBLIN

THE VISIT of Queen Victoria and Prince Albert to
Dublin, which took place in 1849 while I was
residing at Geashill, caused great excitement, for visits of
the sovereign to Ireland have ever been few and far
between. James II. came as a fugitive in 1688. George IV.
arrived in 1821, but was moved thereto by his unpopu-
larity in England. In fact, Victoria was the first monarch
who for very many centuries spontaneously visited this
portion of her dominions with the desire of indicating
her goodwill and her interest in the country. Moreover,
she was young and held universally in high esteem.
Consequently she was welcomed by all classes, and every
one who could manage it went up to Dublin to see her,
and I amongst them.

I shall never forget the scene I witnessed, at her entry, and again on her departure. The enthusiasm of the crowd, composed as it was of all classes, was marvellous. Her public entry was made in the forenoon, and at night the whole city was illuminated, not with gas or electricity as would now be the case, but mainly by candles. A small sconce, holding a lighted candle, was fixed to the frame of each pane of glass in the window, so as to be in a line with the centre of each pane (large plate-glass windows were not then known); and the effect of twelve or sixteen candles alight in a window was very pretty, while a whole street thus lighted up was really striking.

On this occasion every house in every street was thus illuminated. If any had not been illuminated they would have been very quickly smashed. The public buildings, of course, were illuminated by gas devices placed outside.

The whole population turned out at dark to view the illuminations. A party of us, young men and ladies, started in good time, and all went well till we got near the junction of Grafton Street and College Green, where the street becomes narrow. There the crowd was very great, while the roadway was blocked with rows of vehicles of all kinds four or five deep and the side paths packed. We had to stop, progress being impossible.

Just then a crush took place suddenly, and, no doubt, designedly. Ladies screamed, and men pushed and struck one another. One young lady of my party, being pushed off the sidepath, clambered up on the step of an outside hack car packed with men. They were quite civil; they could not make room for her, but held her up, supporting her on her very insecure foothold for some little time, she and they facing each other. The lady I had charge of was lifted clean off her feet in the crush, but was not hurt. Fortunately the crush soon relaxed and we managed to work our way back, for we had only penetrated a little way into the crowd.

But those who had got further down, and all those in carriages, had subsequently a bad time of it, for before ten o'clock it began to rain very heavily, but the crowd could not, or would not disperse. Nor did a single vehicle which had got near the centre of the city—and there were hundreds of them so circumstanced—move for nearly two hours. There sat ladies—many of them dressed up for the occasion, for the day had been very fine—in open carriages or on outside cars in the pelting rain till drenched through, and not a few, when it was possible to move, had a long drive before them ere they reached their homes.

I had to return to the country by an early train in the morning which should have started at seven o'clock. To reach the station I had to cross the whole city. The rain had ceased, but the condition of the streets where the crowd had been dense was indescribable. At that date the streets were not paved, and the roadway was trampled into mud inches deep, and the flagged sidepaths seemed in a very little better state. Everywhere, but especially on the sidepaths, were to be seen bits of cigars, broken pipes, matches and matchboxes, pieces of paper, tattered rags of female attire—many of these of muslin then much worn and other good materials—all trampled into a confused mass of mud and dirt. It reminded one of what a battle-field would look like.

I feared I would be late for my train, for I had great difficulty in getting a car, and only did so by agreeing to share it with others. But I need not have hurried; the train was an hour late in starting, carriage after carriage being added to try and meet the demand for seats. I was so late in arriving at home that I was unable to accomplish my day's work; but no one blamed me.

I went up to Dublin again later on to see the Queen's departure. This proved hardly less adventurous than the illuminations. We drove to Kingstown in an open carriage to see Her Majesty embark. The going was all right, but the return in the dusk was a different matter. The road was crowded with vehicles of all descriptions, outside cars predominating, all bent on getting to the city as quickly as possible. They formed into lines, generally four abreast. But some drivers, who evidently were not abstainers, drove wildly, and sometimes even tried to race and get past those in front. No accident happened to our party, but I was greatly relieved when we neared our destination, for more than once a serious collision seemed inevitable.

Enthusiastic as was her reception. Queen Victoria's distrust of the Irish was not overcome. Many years elapsed ere she re-visited Ireland, and in my opinion her negligence in not doing so was the great mistake of her reign.

During my two years residence in King's County I gained an insight into the character of the Irish peasantry of the South. They differ greatly from those of the northern counties of Ireland. I think what struck me most was their cuteness— indeed, I should say, cunning; and as my youthful appearance led them very justly to assume me to be fair game to practise it on, my opportunities of noticing it were far from being infrequent.

One instance occurred on my going to visit a poor woman who lived in an out-of-the-way place only to be reached on foot. Stopping to inquire the way, I was struck by the extreme civility of a farmer of whom I made the inquiry, and who, not content with pointing out the way, *would* walk with me to show me the way. At this time Father Mathew, the apostle of temperance, was holding meetings all over the country, and administering "the pledge" to numbers of both men and women, many of whom, specially the men, broke it ere long. My conductor brought our conversation round to this subject, and after a while asked my opinion as to the use of whiskey, porter, etc. I replied as best I could, and then he asked me if a glass of porter "would be of any use to him". I replied that I did not think it would do him any harm. Soon after this we parted, and I subsequently learned that he was one of those who, having taken the pledge, repented of having given the promise, and took the opportunity of meeting me to get an opinion which could be so twisted as to enable him to say "a doctor had ordered him to drink porter."

Not long after this I was taken in nicely; a pedlar, who carried a pack containing many miscellaneous articles, came to me one evening when it was nearly dark, and said he was suffering from severe pain in his stomach, and unless he got some relief he could not walk farther. I pitied him, brought him to the dispensary, and gave him a draught to relieve the pain, and then asked my landlady to allow him to sit by the kitchen fire till he got better.

Half an hour elapsed, and then he came to my room door and, knocking, told me he felt nearly quite well, and thanked me profusely for my kindness, adding that he was very sorry he was so poor that he could not pay me anything, but that if only I would accept it, he would give me anything in his pack for half its value. As I had no money to spare, I thanked him, but said I did not want anything; he however would display his wares, offering me one article after another, at what he declared a great loss to him. I tried to get rid of him, but could not.

Finally, he produced a tablecloth, saying he heard I was soon to move into a house of my own, and that this would be so useful; that it had cost him £1, and that I should have it for ten shillings. I objected, but he would have me avail myself of his kindness, and he got the money out of me. When he was gone, my landlady told me that his illness was a pretence, as was his gratitude. Subsequently I found out that the article I had purchased was not worth half the money I had paid him for it. Truly I was a greenhorn!

Although the following incident did not occur till more than twenty years later, when I was master of the Rotunda Hospital, I mention it here: it illustrates a very different phase of Irish character, which amused me much at the time. A patient was sent up to the hospital from the extreme South-west of Ireland by the local medical man. She was barely eighteen years of age, and had a large tumour, probably similar to that of which Queen Mary died, which event brought Elizabeth I to the throne of England.

The only hope of saving this girl's life lay in the performance of a serious operation, but at that date the mortality after these operations was so great—for antiseptics were not yet used or understood—that I was in the habit of postponing the performance of such for as long as possible. This girl was so young, and her general health so good, that I hesitated to operate, and wrote to her father saying I advised him to take her home for six months, at the expiration of which time I would readmit the patient. I explained that, though the operation must be performed, I deemed it wiser to delay it.

In a few days I received a reply from him. It was a most amusing letter and very well written. First he thanked me for my kindness to his daughter, and for saying I would readmit her, but preferred, as an operation must be performed, that it should be done at once, especially as he was too poor to pay the fare for her long journey home and back again. He concluded his letter thus: "Now, sir, I sent up my dear daughter relying on your great skill and in God's mercy. Perform the operation; and whether she lives or dies, I shall be equally satisfied!"

I felt sure that this statement was not intended to convey to me, that he did not care whether his child lived or died, and subsequently I learned that it was quite otherwise, and that he was much attached to her, the more so as the girl was his only child by his first wife who had died soon after her birth, and further that her step-mother, who had several children of her own, was far from kind to her. But the letter, without the knowledge of these facts, was certainly startling. I learned, too, that the man was a schoolmaster and very poorly paid.

I acted in accordance with his wishes, and had the pleasure of sending the girl home in a few weeks perfectly well. The father, poor as he was, sent me up a sack of potatoes as a token of his gratitude, and even paid the carriage!

A few months before I left the country I came across one of the last of the race of men who for a long time were well nigh the only persons who imparted any education to the children of the Irish peasant. I allude to the "hedge schoolmaster," a term I was quite familiar with in my childhood; for though my father had established a school in his parish before I was born, comparatively few availed themselves of it. But I have no recollection of having seen one of these hedge schoolmasters actually teaching till one day, as I was riding home, I saw Some five or six small boys sitting round an old man, under a tall hedge by the roadside not a mile from my house.

I stopped and spoke to him; he seemed ill, and I discovered that he was a great sufferer, so I told him to come to the dispensary. He did so, and I was the means of giving him some temporary relief for which he was most grateful.

He told me what indeed I knew—the condition of the men of his class; that he rarely received any money; that he had spent his life wandering from place to place, teaching when he had the chance the children of the poor the rudiments of learning. This he did in barns, sheds, or by the roadside, receiving in return such scanty food as they had to give, seldom sleeping in a dwelling-house, but in some dilapidated barn or uncleanly shed. In bygone years he had fared better, but now, with schools springing up everywhere, he was no longer wanted.

Poor old man! he soon passed out of my sight. He went his way, I fear, to die a painful death, uncared for, most likely by the wayside, for enter the doors of a poorhouse he would not.

CHAPTER XI

FIRST YEARS OF PROFESSIONAL LIFE IN DUBLIN

Vacant houses in Dublin owing to the famine—I fall overboard and am in great peril—But am hauled on to the wharf—A cautious friend—Other accidents—I take a house in Upper Mount Street —Religion, politics and candidates—I canvass for post of hospital physician, but am defeated— Appointed to the Rotunda Hospital.

ARRIVED IN Dublin I had no difficulty in finding a suitable house, for as a result of the famine many were vacant in every street. But before I took possession of the one selected I met with an accident that might easily have terminated my career, for I fell overboard the mail steamer on a pitch-dark night as she got under way in Kingstown Harbour.

It came about thus. A lady, a relative of mine, and her husband were to cross to Liverpool that night. They had a lot of luggage, and, calling at the house just as they were starting, they asked me to go down to Kingstown and help to get their luggage on board, it having at that time to be carried by porters from the station to the ship—a pretty long walk. I consented, and looked after the luggage while they hurried on board to try and get berths, which, as the voyage occupied over twelve hours, was essential.

There were many passengers, and, a long delay occurring, getting all the luggage on board, the captain got very impatient. I ran below to tell my friend that all was right, to find that gentleman in the middle of a crowd all clamouring for berths which the unfortunate clerk seemed unable to supply. At last I reached him, and he gave me half-a-crown to pay the porter, and up I rushed and made straight for the gangway. I was just fairly on it, when the ship moved and down I went— gangway, stage, and all. It, being iron-bound and furnished with iron handrails on either side, sank like, lead. Fortunately I escaped being entangled; still more fortunate was it that I fell behind the paddle-wheels, for the captain had lost his temper and would not even delay to allow the clerk to land or the stage to be got on shore.

There was a shout, "Man overboard!" The ship stopped, and all was confusion. I was a good swimmer, but the day had been very cold, and I wore a heavy topcoat, had on cloth gloves, and, as I had been riding that afternoon, wore long boots, which, filling with water, weighted me down. It was pitch dark. I turned towards the quay which stood fifteen feet perpendicularly above me, and saw nothing to lay hold of. I then turned towards the ship, and called for a rope. They shouted that there was one out from the ship. I said that I could not see it. Then a flambeau was held over her side. I saw the rope and was able to reach it; having the half-crown in my hand, I tried to put it into my mouth, but the salt water got in also, so the half-crown had to be let go!

A minute or two elapsed—it seemed to me hours—when a lifebuoy was flung from the shore; but it fell so far from me that I dare not let go the rope, and I shouted that I could not swim so far. Another was thrown; it fell close to me and I reached it. It was shaped like a dumb-bell, with a stout rope attached to its centre. So by seizing the rope I was able to get first one and then the other leg over it, and was hoisted on to the pier, sticking out my feet to save myself from being torn or bruised by the rough stones of which the wall was built. Great cheering welcomed me as I scrambled on to dry land, and the porters showed me great kindness, bringing me to their hut close by, in which there was a good fire, fortunately, as I was very cold.

Then the question arose as to how I should get home in my dripping state. My friend's coachman was on the pier, he having brought down horses which his master was taking to England—horses were carried on the mail boats in those days. He, of course, came to my assistance, and I sent him to the house of an old gentleman who lived near, asking him to lend me dry clothes which would be returned next day.

The old gentleman feared he was being imposed upon, especially as he did not know that I had come to Dublin. However, he sent the clothes by his own servant, with directions that he was not to part with them unless sure of my identity. That was easily settled, but the clothes—well, they did not exactly fit me! I was not tall, but the old man was much shorter, and what he wanted in height was amply compensated for in breadth. The band of his trousers went about twice round one. The figure I must have cut when clad in his rather ancient suit may be imagined; however, it was dark and no one minded me much. I was none the worse for the ducking, but I had a narrow escape of being drowned.

I was the third person to whom a very similar accident had happened much about this time; one was a gentleman I knew something of. He was going on board a steamer which was about to sail from the North Wall Quay, Dublin; his foot slipped, and he fell into the river and was drowned. The other was a well-known man; he fell into the sea at Holyhead while in the act of boarding a steamer; he, too, was drowned. I alone of the three escaped. I, of course, was young; they were elderly. I know not whether they could swim or not. To God's mercy I owe the life then spared.

I hardly know what my ideas as for my future were when a small house in Upper Mount Street received me as tenant in October, 1850. I was very far from being sanguine of succeeding in Dublin, and knew that most likely I should have to seek an opening in some smaller sphere, like many others I knew of. In the meantime I hoped to gain experience and a better knowledge of my profession. Looking back now over my life, now prolonged beyond four-score years, I see clearly how I was guided by God's providence in every step, thwarting me in obtaining objects I desired, and opening my way in a direction which, though at the time quite other than I wished, led in the end to professional success such as I had never deemed possible.

I was, of course, anxious to be attached to some hospital where I would have the opportunity of gaining experience in the treatment of the sick; so not long after coming up to town, learning that the guardians of the South Dublin Union had decided, in consequence of the vast number of poor seeking admission to their hospital, to appoint an additional assistant physician, I became a candidate, and as I was fortunate enough to obtain the support of a gentleman who devoted much of his time to the affairs of the union, I was hopeful of success.

In this instance, as, indeed, in all others in Ireland, religion and politics played an important part in the election. There were some twenty or more candidates, and there were consequently several rounds of voting, those candidates who obtained the fewest votes being on each occasion thrown out, till their number was reduced to three, namely, a Roman Catholic gentleman, a Nonconformist, and myself. Hitherto, I had on each occasion headed the list, and did so on the semi-final round, when the Roman Catholic, having obtained the fewest votes, was thrown out; and I, turning to him asked, "Who will your friends now vote for?" he replied, "Against you, as you are the Conservative candidate," which, in truth, I was not, the result being that I was defeated by just one vote. The result of that election again influenced my whole career. I had always wished to be a physician, and to be attached as such to a general hospital. Instead, I was destined to take up a special department of the profession of medicine.

During my canvass I had called on one of my former teachers, Dr. Charles Johnston, who had been master of the Rotunda Hospital when I was a pupil there, and asked him to assist me. He received me very kindly, but replied that any interest he possessed he had promised to another; but he immediately added, "I will help you in another direction. I can obtain for you the appointment of assistant to the master of the Rotunda Hospital which will be vacant in a few months, and I advise you to accept it." He proceeded to tell me that it had been promised to him for his son, but as the latter had decided to give up medicine and enter the Church, he could have the nomination transferred to me.

Being at the time hopeful that I should be successful

at the approaching election, I said I would like to have a
little time to consider the matter; but on my being
defeated, at once called on him, and told him I would
gladly accept his kind offer. In doing so I was influenced
solely by the feeling that I would thus have the opportunity of improving my professional knowledge; but, in
point of fact it led, though not till twenty years elapsed,
to my being elected master of the Rotunda Hospital, a
position worthy of being the object of any man's
ambition, and one which at the time I am speaking of, it
never entered into my head I could ever attain.

CHAPTER XII

SLOW PROGRESS IN DUBLIN

Anxious years—Marriage and a family, but only a small income— Tempted to go to England—My wife opposed—Join the staff of the Adelaide Hospital—I make progress and publish my lectures to students—Rapid success—A great compliment— Master of the Rotunda Hospital—A magnificent monument to Dr. Mosse—What one man can do—Inception and growth of the hospital— Lotteries to raise funds—Building a chapel as a source of income!—Other strange methods—I find the hospital deficient in modern and sanitary conveniences, and commence reforms.

THE YEARS that followed were fall of anxiety. I married young, children came, but my income remained miserably small, I am convinced that not one of my contemporaries had such a struggle or met so many disappointments as I did. So slow was my progress in gaining patients that, after being in Dublin seven or eight years, I, on two occasions, entered into negotiations, with the view of joining as partner, gentlemen in practice in England. On the second occasion I had nearly closed with the offer made me, when my wife begged me to wait for one year more before deciding to move, pointing out that we were free from debt, and. asking me to trust God's guidance. I agreed to wait, and ere the year expired things looked brighter.

The monotony of my professional life, consisting as it did for many years in a struggle to make the two ends meet, was unexpectedly broken in 1868 by my being invited to join the staff of the Adelaide Hospital, a small ward for the reception of patients suffering from those diseases, treatment of which I had made a special study, being allotted to me. I had no idea that such an appointment was contemplated. I, of course, jumped at the offer, which, as it proved, had a marked effect on my future.

From the first my beds were filled, and I had not infre-quently to trespass on the kindness of my colleagues, who would lend me a bed for some interesting case. Although it never was directly stated to me, I believe the invitation to join the staff was due to the kindness of the two physicians to the hospital, Dr. James Little and Dr. Henry Head, to whom I know I owe much besides.

I soon had a large extern clinic, and at once commenced giving clinical lectures, which were much appreciated by the class. They were attended by pupils from other hospitals also. After a time some of the class asked me to publish these, which, though I had only very rough notes to guide me, I did. They appeared in the *Medical Press,* at that time edited by the late Dr. Arthur Jacob, and I had an edition of 500 copies reprinted from this, every one of which, to my great surprise, were sold in a few months. A second and third enlarged editions followed, the latter being reprinted in America and also translated into French. Altogether there were seven large editions published in Great Britain. Then, though pressed by the publishers to issue another, I decided not to do so, for so greatly had our knowledge of the causation of these diseases advanced, and so improved had our methods of treatment become, that it would have been necessary to rewrite a great part of the work, a task for which I had neither the time nor inclination.

I was much struck by an incident which occurred in connection with the sale of the first copies. The publisher was a medical bookseller in Dublin whom I knew very well, and the bookbinder being dilatory I called on him, with the result that he promised to send a batch of the volumes to the publisher without further delay. So I called at the shop to find out if he had kept his promise. The publisher told me that he had, adding, "And I have sold a copy already." This was at about twelve o'clock in the day. Of course I asked who it was he had sold it to, but he refused to tell me, adding, "The books were delivered late yesterday afternoon, and they were being placed on the counter just before we closed, when a medical man you know very well came. While he was being served he asked what books they were. I told him it was a book you were publishing, and he then said, 'I would not trust one word that man wrote,' taking up as he spoke one of the volumes, which he looked over for a few minutes, then laying it down said, 'I will not buy the book, but if you will lend it me I would like to look it over, and I promise you to bring it back safe tomorrow morning.' I lent it him, and this morning he came in saying he would keep the book, and paid for it." I consider that the greatest compliment I was ever paid, for though I was never told his name, I am sure I know who it was—a man with whom, though at one time my colleague, I never got on friendly terms.

My connection with the Adelaide Hospital ceased on my being elected master of the Rotunda Hospital in November, 1878. Then followed the busiest years of my life. I had already a large consulting practice, and to this was now added the charge of a great hospital.

The position of master of the Rotunda Hospital is a peculiar one. It can be held for seven years only, and he must reside in the hospital, a handsome suite of apartments being allotted to him. He has no colleague, and is consequently personally responsible for every patient in it. He has, however, two assistants, who are nominated by him, but their appointment must be confirmed by the governors. The governors can reject the person nominated by the master, but they cannot elect an assistant unless he be nominated by him. The whole responsibility, therefore, as to the assistant's fitness rests on the master.

Nor do his duties end in merely treating the patients committed to his care. He is a governor, and, in fact, very much in the position of managing director of a large establishment. The secretary will come to him for advice or instructions, as will also the matron—at least, it was so in my time, though I should hope that the reorganisation which was initiated by me and which was carried out under my successors will have relieved him of much that devolved on me. It was only by the most methodical arrangement of my time that I was able to get through my daily work.

I had, besides, a good deal of literary work on hand, to accomplish which I devoted three hours, 8 to 11 p.m., regularly. I never sat up after the latter hour. I commenced my morning visit to the wards at 9 a.m. punctually. The work, too, became heavier, in consequence of the governors, on my suggestion, converting a large detached wing of the institution into an auxiliary hospital for the treatment of chronic affections, many of the patients admitted into it needing the performance of capital operations which often occupied much time. This department had not existed previously.

The Rotunda Hospital is a magnificent monument of the philanthropy of one man, and of his wonderful energy and perseverance in overcoming difficulties which would appear insuperable to most men. But Dr. Mosse was by himself. While still a young man his compassion was excited, by witnessing the suffering and the neglected conditions of the poor during childbirth. At his own cost he took a house in South Georges Street, Dublin, then known as Georges Lane. The house was small and soon proved altogether insufficient for the purpose intended, which was the reception of women during their confinements, so, with the aid of some subscriptions he succeeded in obtaining, he took the adjoining one also; but this addition proved wholly inadequate to meet the demand for admission, and he boldly resolved to build a lying-in hospital, which would not only be a charitable institution of the most useful character, but also an ornament to the city.

He commenced operations by acquiring the site on which the hospital and public rooms now stand. From the shape of the principal public room the hospital acquired the name of "Rotunda," by which it is so widely known. The ground behind, which was subsequently laid out as a pleasure ground, forms the Rotunda Gardens. Then, though he had not £500 in the world, he commenced building a hospital, the architect's estimated cost of which was no less than £20,000!

At that date, 1745, many of the Irish nobility had houses in Dublin, where they resided some months during each year, as did also many of the country gentry. Dr. Mosse succeeded in gaining the patronage of these, and, what was of even more importance, handsome donations of money. The Lord Lieutenant favoured him, and the foundation stone was laid with great ceremony.

So far he had succeeded marvellously, but his difficulties were only beginning, and though subscriptions came in, the expenditure was so heavy that his funds were soon exhausted. He pledged his credit to its utmost limits, but even this money so raised was soon gone. Then he appealed to the Irish parliament, pointing out that the institution was truly a national one. A grant of money was made, and after it was opened £3,000 was for many years voted towards its support.

But the doctor's difficulties were far from being surmounted. He had recourse to lotteries (then legal), from which he derived considerable sums; but he was always struggling with debt, for which he was frequently threatened with arrest—indeed I believe on at least one occasion he actually was arrested. But he never faltered in his purpose. It was ten years ere the hospital was completed. In 1756 it was incorporated by Royal Charter, the Lord Lieutenant being named president, and Dr. Mosse, as was right, nominated the first master. He was to hold office for life.

But his labours did not end with the completion of the hospital; he wanted to have it, in at least a great degree, independent of donations and subscriptions. His first step was to have a chapel opened in the building, which he hoped to fill with a wealthy congregation. It exists still, though I regret to say it has ceased to bring an income to the charity. It is really handsome. The pews are of mahogany, as are the pillars that support the gallery, in which is an organ, said to have been taken from a ship forming part of the Spanish Armada, which was wrecked on the coast of Ireland. The ceiling is beautiful, decorated with stucco work done by an Italian Dr. Mosse had discovered and brought over to Ireland,

The same artist also decorated the houses of many of the nobility and gentry who lived in the neighbourhood of the hospital, at that time the fashionable end of the city. These houses are now either public offices or have degenerated into tenement dwellings.

The chapel was at first a great success, every pew being rented by people of wealth and position, and it was the fashion to go there. All that has changed long since, but my mother, who was at school in a street adjacent to the hospital at the time of the union, often told me when I was a child of the fetes and promenades which were held in the Rotunda Gardens when she was a girl, little dreaming that her child was to live to be the head of the institution.

Dr. Mosse then decided to set about building public rooms on the ground adjoining the hospital, believing that these, a need for which existed in the city, would produce an income for its support. The "Rotunda," or "Round Room," as it is generally called, paid well from the first, it being in demand for balls, concerts, public meetings, etc., the other rooms also being much used. But fashion moved to the south side of the city, where other rooms have been built, so the income derived is now but small. Moreover, money to complete the buildings failing, debentures chargeable on them, and which still exist, were issued, the interest thereon being paid by the governors. The upkeep, too, is an expensive item.

When I was elected master, the hospital had been in existence for a hundred years, but from causes into which it is needless to enter it had changed but little in its internal arrangements and management during that time. The other Dublin hospitals had been vastly improved and modernised, but when I went back to the Rotunda as master, twenty years after I had left it as assistant, to my surprise I found little, indeed scarcely anything, changed in the interval.

An ample supply of water at high pressure had been brought into the city, and introduced into the hospital, but not into the wards. There was no means of giving a patient a bath, nor was there proper provision made for the attendants even to wash their hands. Further, I found that extensive repairs were needed, especially to the public rooms, and many alterations, some of them structural, urgently required to improve the sanitary conditions. Worst of all, I found that there was no money available, but that, on the contrary, there was an overdraft due to the "the bank amounting to nearly £1,000. Indeed, debt was steadily increasing, for the income of the institution did not suffice to meet the expenditure. The 'governors did not seem to know anything about these matters.

CHAPTER XIII

IMPROVING THE
ROTUNDA HOSPITAL

A week or two after my election, a sermon was to be preached in the chapel in aid of the funds of the hospital; and I spoke to the clergyman, asking him to say that its needs were so great and its financial position so bad, that not less than £3,000 were required, and that immediately. Among those who chanced to be present on that occasion was the late Mr. Samuel Adair, a well-known and much respected gentleman.

After the conclusion of the service Mr. Adair came to me and put several questions relative to these matters, which I was able to answer to his satisfaction. He immediately gave us a handsome donation, agreed to become a governor, and from that day on took an active part in the management of the hospital. Indeed, it was in a great degree owing to his support that I was able to have much that was needful accomplished during my seven years' tenure of office.

The first thing we did was to get an architect's report as to needful repairs and alterations. A small committee was appointed to consider this and to devise the means of raising funds.

I need hardly say that with respect to the latter the work devolved entirely on myself. I engaged a clerk temporarily, who copied letters dictated by me, which I signed by the dozen. The responses to these were wonderfully satisfactory. In these letters was usually enclosed a handbill of which a copy is printed (p. 145). I give it as affording a brief outline of the history of the hospital and of the claims it then, as now, has on the public.

By means of appeals to the public, and lastly, by a bazaar, held in the Round Room, a considerable sum of money was raised, and many improvements were effected, the most difficult task being to try and improve the basement story, which was, and, I fear, must ever remain, very dark, and was at that time also ill-ventilated; but we succeeded in letting in a good deal of light and air. All those matters were willingly sanctioned by the governors. But when it came to providing suitable premises for the treatment of extern patients, of whom a large number daily presented themselves, and the organ-

ROTUNDA HOSPITAL

FOR POOR LYING-IN WOMEN,

AND FOR

The Treatment of Diseases Peculiar to Women.

FOUNDED IN 1745, INCORPORATED BY ROYAL CHARTER IN 1756.

MORE than a hundred years ago, Dr. Bartholomew Mosse conceived the idea of rearing an Hospital which would be at once a refuge for poor suffering women, and a great School of Obstetric Medicine. With untiring energy he carried out his great plan ; he died in poverty, but his memory has ever been revered as one of the greatest benefactors of suffering humanity.

Nor was he content with erecting a magnificent hospital ; he sought also to create an income for its future support ; but his efforts in this respect only serve as a proof of the fallacy of man's foresight. His provision for the future maintenance of the hospital was to be derived mainly from four sources—

1st. A tax imposed by Act of Parliament on "public sedan chairs."
2nd. A Government grant of £3,000 a year.
3rd. The profits derived from letting the Rotunda and adjoining ground.
4th. A tax imposed on the inhabitants of the square, in consideration of which the Governors were bound to light it.

As "public sedan chairs" are things of the past, the tax is no longer a source of income ; but, unfortunately, a sum of £11,000 was borrowed, chargeable on this tax, and the interest, amounting to £440 a year, has still to be paid by the hospital.

Next, Government has gradually reduced the Grant to £700, and this is continued solely on the ground of the great *national* benefit conferred by the hospital as an educational establishment.

Third. The profits derived from the public rooms and gardens, at one time very large, have of late fallen off, specially since the opening of the Exhibition Palace.

Fourth. The square tax, too, has ceased to produce a revenue. The point having been raised that the lighting should be by oil lamps, not *by gas !* the question is still *sub judice ;* so we can only say that for the present the charity loses this source of income.

Thus this excellent charity, this renowned school of medicine, which for more than a hundred years has attracted numbers of pupils, *Male and Female*, from all parts of the world, has gradually had its sources of income lessened. The result is that the institution is this day in debt to an extent not much under £1,000. Nor is this all. Time has told on its fabric ; it needs extensive repairs, especially the wing in which are situated the wards devoted to the treatment of the diseases peculiar to women. In fact £3,000 must be promptly expended in repairs and improvements, or the building will fall to decay.

Can any one read this outline of the history of this renowned hospital without feeling a wish to aid it ? Its claims are of no common nature. They are those of a charity and of a school of obstetric medicine of which the country is justly proud. As a charity it annually relieves thousands of the suffering poor, while to the wealthy classes its existence is no less valuable, since from the experience obtained within its walls the wives and daughters of the rich derive the greatest benefit.

This Hospital affords shelter and relief on an average to 2,000 poor women annually, excluding those admitted into the chronic wards ; a large number of women are attended at their own homes, while over 3,000 patients are treated during the year in the Dispensary which is attached to the Hospital.

You are earnestly entreated to contribute to the Fund now being raised, in order to prevent such a National loss and National disgrace, as the decay of this great Institution would be.

Annual Subscriptions are also earnestly solicited.

Donations and Subscriptions will be received by LOMBE ATTHILL, M.D., Master of the Hospital ; by Mr. MULLEN, Secretary, Rotunda Hospital ; or by any of the Governors.

ising the extern maternity, opposition came, I regret to say that it was led by the medical members of the board.

The master for the time being is an *ex officio* governor, but ceases to be so at the expiration of his term of office, but is usually re-elected a governor subsequently. There were four ex-master governors at the date of my election. One, Dr. Evory Kennedy, never attended the meetings of the board. I had the misfortune to have failed to gain at my election the support of any one of the others, but we were nevertheless very good friends, and from Dr. Alfred McClintock I received the heartiest support in the carrying out of the various improvements I have referred to; but when it was proposed to erect a small building for the use of extern patients, being afraid of increasing the debt, he opposed it on the grounds of want of funds. Another of the "ex-masters opposed it, and also the extension of the extern maternity department, as unnecessary, and as calculated to induce patients to remain at their homes for their confinements instead of seeking admission into the hospital. The result has proved to have had quite the opposite effect, for as the numbers attended in their own homes increased, more patients sought admission to the lying-in wards.

The board met one morning to consider the architect's report. It was divided into two parts. The first part related to many matters I have spoken of and to alterations in what was known as the "auxiliary hospital," and which I urged the board to convert into one for the treatment of the diseases peculiar to women, instead of using the wards in it for lying-in patients. All these matters were approved, and the work ordered to be proceeded with. The second part related to a new building of very moderate dimensions, mainly for dispensary work, which has long given place to the fine hospital erected subsequently, mainly, indeed nearly altogether, through the exertions of Dr. (now Sir William) Smyly, during his mastership.

Dr. McClintock, who was present at the meeting of the board, approved of the first part of the report, but when the second part was reached he pushed back his chair, and, rising, moved the adjournment of the meeting. I begged the governors to wait and consider the rest of the report, and as there was further opposition, I asked them at least to walk round and see the apartment in which these patients were being treated. This they agreed to do. It happened to be a very cold, raw morning in February. Now the only place where these extern patients could he seen was in a small room off the porters lodge, about 10 ft. by 8 ft. in size. There was no fireplace, and the assistant on duty, in order to have some warmth for himself and the poor patients, used to have a small petroleum stove burning, which always Smoked horridly. Then there was no waiting room for the patients, and they had to stand in a narrow, dark passage leading to the little room.

The governors, some eight or nine in number, followed me into this dark passage, and found themselves wedged in amongst some twenty poor, and certainly not very cleanly women, who were watching for the door to open and admit the one nearest. With some difficulty I got through the crowd, opened the door, and introduced the governor nearest to me, who happened to be the late Mr. C. Uniacke Townshend. He stepped in and saw the then assistant sitting enveloped in an overcoat near the petroleum stove, the room being filled with the pungent fumes therefrom. Mr. Townshend stepped back more quickly than he had entered, saying, "That's enough; let us go back to the board-room." I believe one or two more-governors looked in, withdrawing speedily. This bringing of the governors to see the place was quite unpremeditated, but it answered the purpose admirably. The architect's plans were approved, Dr. McClintock contenting himself by merely having a resolution passed that the new work was not to be undertaken till the money for the purpose was provided. The board then adjourned for a month. Before that time elapsed we had succeeded in collecting some more money—not a sufficient sum to meet the intended outlay, but I was determined that the new building should be put in hand at once. So, to meet the difficulty caused by the resolution referred to, I got the bank to agree to advance if needed any sum up to £1,000 to the governors on my sole

guarantee, the governors neither personally nor collec-
tively to be responsible for such advances. I laid a letter
from the bank to this effect before the board, and they
then at once ordered the work to be put in hand. As a
matter of fact, the whole sum needed was raised by one
means or another, without the bank being called on to
make any advance. And further, before my term as master
of the hospital expired, not only had the previously
existing debt been wiped out, but, moreover, the
governors had a considerable credit balance in bank. It
remained for Sir William J. Smyly to carry much further
what I very imperfectly began, and to make the Rotunda
by far the most complete and perfect hospital for women
in the kingdom. Without doubt, second only to the
founder, Dr. Bartholomew Mosse, the public and the
profession alike owe to him a great debt of gratitude.

The efforts made by the governors to improve the
hospital benefited all the Dublin hospitals, for, having
appealed to the corporation for a grant of money, that
body appointed a committee to meet a deputation from
the board. They gave us a kindly reception and acceded
to our application. Other hospitals, on hearing of our
success, also applied for aid, and since that date the
corporation has voted a sum of, I think, £2,000 annually,
which is divided amongst the various city hospitals.
Further, the paving of the streets having commenced
about this time, I appealed to the paving committee,

requesting them to pave with wood the part of the street in front and on the west side of the hospital, pointing out the serious harm the rattle of vehicles over the stone setts, specially in the early morning, would have on patients, many of whom must always be seriously ill. They agreed, though not to the needful extent to my request, and in like manner paved with wood those parts of streets which ran in front of other hospitals. I am pleased to think that I was thus the means of benefiting many sufferers. But apart from alterations and improvements in the structure, the internal arrangements needed to be remodelled, and that was a far more difficult thing to effect.

There was not a trained nurse in the hospital with the exception of the head nurse, and she, though an excellent woman, was one of the regular old school, and intensely conservative. The question of how to effect what was necessary, namely, a complete change in the nursing staff, perplexed me greatly. I could not think of discharging a number of women who had filled the post of ward nurses for a considerable time, and who for the most part were well conducted, if illiterate. Indeed, one or two had become careful and experienced nurses.

The mode of appointing nurses, too, was most objectionable, while their pay was shamefully small. To begin with the matron—she was a nice old lady, a widow who had formerly been in a good social position—she wished to do right, but had no previous training of any kind, and not the most remote idea of what the duties of the matron of a hospital should be; in fact, she was a house-keeper, not a matron. When a vacancy occurred for a ward nurse she was in the habit of looking out for a respectable middle-aged woman, generally an old servant, who was installed in her ward without as much as one day's previous training, and she got none in the hospital, for the matron knew no more than herself. The head nurse's duties were virtually wholly confined to the super-vision of the women who were admitted to be trained as monthly nurses and midwives.

It was easy to say, "Put an end to that system," but what to do with the existing staff was the difficulty. The wage paid to the nurses was but ten pounds a year each. That, I greatly fear, was supplemented by money extracted from the patients, though this was strictly forbidden. One, indeed, and she the senior of the whole staff, I felt sure, did this habitually, but I could not prove it. Further, their laundry was not provided for, so they washed their underclothes in their wards; as to their dresses, they were never washed. They provided their own clothes and all wore black dresses always.

In this dilemma I decided in the first place to ask the board to raise the wages of all the nurses; to allow me to divide them into three classes, the first class to have £20, the two other proportionally less. The board acceded to my recommendation, and I selected two, not the longest in the hospital, but the most intelligent and most trust-worthy of the twelve ward nurses, for the first class. It turned out as I expected; several of the others finding themselves passed over were dissatisfied, even though their wages had been raised, especially the senior one already alluded to. She afterwards intimated that if the board would give her a gratuity she would resign. This was done, and her place filled by a woman of a very superior class.

One by one the illiterate, one of whom, at least, could not read, were got rid of. Washing in the wards was strictly prohibited, all the nurses' clothes being sent to the laundry.

But an unexpected difficulty arose when I announced that the wearing of black dresses would not any longer be permitted, the board having at my request undertaken to supply the nurses with uniform made of a washing material. They disliked the idea greatly, but an accidental occurrence helped me just at this juncture. The Lord Lieutenant announced his intention of visiting the hospital, of which he was *ex officio* president of the board of governors.

We had just five days' notice of his Excellency's intention; then, all being anxious to make a good appearance on the occasion, the making of the uniforms was hurried up, some of the nurses even offering, if given the material, to have them made for themselves. So we succeeded in having all the ward nurses dressed up in time to receive his Excellency and the Marchioness of Abercorn, the latter of whom took the greatest interest in the institution. Though the nurses disliked giving up the well-worn black dresses, they said nothing to me, and the enthusiasm which the Viceregal visit excited helped to smooth matters. But I met with opposition from our old, and, indeed, for many reasons, respected head nurse. She had been in office for some twenty-five years, and though she was glad to see improvements effected, disliked changes in old-established customs. She objected to the female pupils, who were specially under her supervision, being obliged to wear a uniform.

She thought it derogatory, though she did not say that openly to me, but she did ask me "not to require the poor things to wear a cold calico dress in winter." Of course her appeal was in vain, but not one of them would go outside the door of the hospital wearing it. Thus one day I was summoned to see a lady who was taken suddenly ill in an hotel only a minute or two's walk from the hospital, finding, on visiting her, that I needed the immediate assistance of a nurse, I wrote to the head to send over at once one of her pupils. She arrived quickly, but to my dismay dressed in black. I asked her why she came so dressed, and she replied that "she could not walk across the street in her nurse's uniform"!

This incident shows the difficulties which I had to

contend with in carrying out even the most obviously reasonable reforms, and why more was not effected by me. It was not till eight or nine years had elapsed that, during the mastership of Dr., now Sir William, Smyly, who had been my assistant during the latter part of my term, the posts of matron and head nurse were abolished, an efficient lady superintendent appointed, and the nursing staff organised, as in all well-managed hospitals.

To Sir William Smyly great credit is further due for the success of his efforts to have a new gynaecological hospital built, for the reception of chronic cases now known as "the Cairnes Wing." The old house which I had induced the governors to convert to this purpose was unsuitable in view of modem requirements. It had originally been an asylum for the blind, and though it stood close to, it did not stand on the hospital property. The governors had been forced to buy it many years ago in self-defence, as it was about to be licensed as a public-house. It was connected with the hospital by an open corridor, and, till I became master, had always been known as "The Blind House." Then it was named, I think, on Dr. McClintock's suggestion, "The Auxiliary Hospital." It is now used as a residence for intern pupils. The present master, Dr. Hastings Tweedy, also has signalised his term of office by inducing the board to erect a building which provides rooms for the nurses and accommodation for ladies studying medicine.

The Rotunda is now the most complete, as it is the largest, hospital for women in the United Kingdom. Over 2,000 patients are on an average admitted annually into the lying-in wards. Over 2,000 more are attended at their own homes in connection with the extern maternity department, which I had the good fortune to establish. Some 500 cases of chronic disease are admitted each year into the Cairnes Wing, many of these requiring operations of the greatest magnitude, while the number of poor women treated daily in the dispensary is very large.

All honour be to the memory of Dr. Bartholomew Mosse, who originated the scheme, devised the plan, raised the money, and lived to see built this fine hospital. He died impoverished, and his life was shortened in consequence of his anxieties, cares, and worries; but his memory will live as long as the massive walls of his hospital stand, and he will be honoured as one who has conferred the greatest benefits, not alone on the poor of Dublin or of Ireland, but on the human race in many climes, where the knowledge acquired within its walls has been employed by thousands of medical men for the relief of the sufferer and for the saving of life.

As an example of distances from which students come to study at the Rotunda Hospital I may mention that I have a copy of a photograph taken in 1881 of the then intern pupils in a group, with the name and address of' each of them written underneath. The latter reads as follows: Cork, Derry, Kingstown, Copenhagen, London, Buenos Ayres, Monte Video, Bengal, United States, Leeds, Edinburgh, Cork"; and this list is nowise exceptional, though the localities from which they come may vary greatly. Before the civil war in America, many students came from the southern States of the Union. They were invariably such nice, gentlemanly men, but slavery was a subject not to be touched on. Few came from the northern States. One of these was an amusing character, he must have been over thirty, and was a married man. Evidently his education had been of the most imperfect nature, but his industry was unbounded. He made, too, the quaintest remarks. He had taken a great fancy to me, and wanted me to go back with him. One day he said, "Come to Alabama, doctor, with me; you will just drop down there, and pop up straight like a cork." Another time he said, "Doctor, I have been ten years in practice, but I tell you, till recently it was all poking in the dark with me." Poor fellow! I wonder what became of him when the tide of civil war swept over his country. It was while I was assistant that this incident occurred.

CHAPTER XIV

I GIVE UP PRACTICE AND RECEIVE HONOURS

*Withdrawing gradually—Elected president of the College of Physicians—
Elected representative on the General Medical Council— I give a
banquet—A part of the press resents my invitation to the Lord
Lieutenant—I come in for abuse—A clever and amusing leading article—I
give a lift to a political opponent—"Three acres and a cow" is first
uttered—An amusing allusion.*

MY SEVEN YEARS' term of office passed rapidly.
During it I relinquished much of the most
laborious part of my professional work, and as time
passed on, still more; till, after the exploration of fifty
years' of strenuous professional life, I withdrew altogether
from practice.

Before doing so the Fellows of the College of
Physicians honoured me by electing me their president,
and a little later also elected me their representative on
the General Medical Council, a seat on which I occupied
for fourteen years. Then advancing age and its usual
results led me to resign.

While president I gave a banquet in the college hall,

which his Excellency the Lord lieutenant honoured with his presence. There were more than a hundred guests present.

Party feeling was at that time running very high, and my action in inviting his Excellency was subsequently adversely commented on by a section of the press, specially as in his speech, when responding to the toast of his health, his Excellency strayed on to over-delicate ground, taking the opportunity of denying the truth of a statement which had been made in certain papers to the effect that a misunderstanding existed between him and the Chief Secretary, Mr. Arthur Balfour.

The next morning there appeared in the national papers violent criticisms of this speech, and, as already mentioned, I came in for a share of the abuse. This I looked upon as not only unfair, but a grave mistake on the critics' part, because in proposing the health, I said "that politics had no place in the college." Of course I took no public notice of the articles. Great, then, was my surprise to receive, some days later, a copy of *The Nation,* a very ably-conducted weekly paper of extreme political bias, and on opening it to find that, instead of being blamed, I was praised.

The leading article was not only very cleverly written, but also very amusing. I have that paper still, and must quote a passage from it.

Beginning with a wicked attack on his Excellency, it

proceeds to say: "The Viceroy, according to himself, has never been regarded in his proper light, Ireland, curiously enough, has persisted in regarding him as the Chief Secretary's Castle lackey, but the Lord Lieutenant has now been enabled to set public opinion right.

"When the great Napoleon accomplished his famous descent upon the plains of Italy, he made the passage of the precipitous and dangerous Alpine passes safely, but ungloriously, on a dull, slow-paced mountain donkey. When, however, the period of triumph came and the imperial diadem pressed his brow, the painter David represented the Emperor mounted on a fiery Arabian steed performing impossible feats of horsemanship on the slippery slopes of ice.

"Somewhat similar in effect has been the portrait-painting of his Excellency. The majority of the people of Ireland have been picturing the Chief Secretary as painfully struggling through the dangerous defiles of Irish difficulties, with the aid of an ass, but now it seems that the ass was a spirited charger and never owned a rider at all.

"Wondrous change! It matters nothing to the Lord Lieutenant that Dr. Atthill, the eminent and courteous president of the great and distinguished institution which entertained his Lordship, had virtually warned him, when introducing his name to the assembled guests, that, though living in a time when politics had assumed a most virulent complexion and party spirit ran high, yet in that

Hall politics were unknown, his Excellency would take no hint."

Much as I was amused by reading this article, much more was I astonished at finding myself spoken of as being "eminent and courteous," and I could not imagine who the writer could be. The paper was one I hardly ever saw, and I did not know who the editor was. During the day I made inquiries, and learned that it was owned and edited by Mr. T. D. Sullivan, one of a very talented family. This information gave me a clue to the kindly reference to myself.

During the previous summer I had resided in a house situated on the south side of the promontory of Howth, some ten miles from Dublin, and I used to go into town every morning by an early train. The railway station being three miles from the house, I had to drive down. The last mile of the road ran close to the seashore, and was devoid of any shelter. On one very inclement morning I drove down as usual in a wagonette. I always drove myself, so sat in front, the servant being seated beside me, and as it was pouring rain, and no one else was going with me, I ordered the cushions to be taken off the back part of the vehicle and left them behind.

It was blowing a gale in our faces, and just as I reached the most exposed part of the road I saw in front of me a gentleman dressed in a black frock coat, trying to defend himself from the rain and struggling to make headway against the storm. As soon as I came up with him, I pulled up and said, "Sir, if you do not mind sitting on a seat without cushions I shall be happy to give you a lift." He thanked me as he got in, as he also did on reaching the station, where we arrived just in time to catch the train.

A day or two after, this gentleman came on the platform where I was standing and bowed courteously to me. As I did not know who he was, I turned to a porter and asked who that gentleman was. He replied, "Sure, that is Mr. Sullivan." Evidently I had taken "an angel unawares" into my carriage on the preceding day, and months after was repaid by his kind allusion to me in his paper. I never met him subsequently.

This reminds me that about a year previously to this incident I had heard him make one of the aptest after-dinner speeches I ever remember. It was at a dinner given by the members of the Royal Hibernian Academy, on the evening preceding their opening day, at which I was a guest. Mr. Sullivan at that time filled the office of Lord Mayor of Dublin, and as such his health was proposed by the chairman. It was not very long after a hotly contested general election, during which a candidate, I think it was Mr. Jesse Collings, in a speech advocating the claims of agricultural labourers and the necessity of encouraging the allotment of land to them, declared that in his opinion every such man should have "three acres and a cow." The saying caught on, and was frequently quoted. Well, Mr. Sullivan in his speech returning thanks, after alluding to advantages which followed the cultivation of art, etc., paused for a moment, and then, speaking slowly and with much solemnity, said to this effect: "I am aware that in this room politics or any allusion to politics are forbidden, but with regret I feel I must break through this rule, for looking around me, I am filled with the desire to be the possessor of "three acres and a cow," pointing, as he spoke, to a painting hanging close by, representing a cow quietly feeding on green pasture in-close contiguity to a pretty cottage. I never had heard greater applause or such hearty laughter as followed. I believe he and his talented brother are both long since dead.

CHAPTER XV

A RETROSPECT

The cares and trials of a medical man—Ungrateful patients—And grateful—Patients who make a change—A revolution in the practice of medicine—Sulphuric ether—Recollections of leading men—Some anecdotes—The lady's shilling fee—Sir Dominic Corrigan—The fat surgeon and the thin, and the highwayman—Some more stories—My many friends—Compensations.

I FOUND IT nearly as difficult to give up practice as it had been at one time to gain it. It was with real reluctance that I had to refuse to see patients, for many of whom I felt a sincere regard, and whose welfare I desired.: A medical man's life is ever full of cares and worries, disappointments, failures, and successes; the slow growth of practice, the disappointment of not being employed by persons you expected would do so, the discovery that a patient leaves you in favour of another you may believe to be less worthy of confidence than yourself, are trials for beginners and are even felt by seniors. But such things are inevitable.

Then the anxiety about serious cases, and the painful feeling of disappointment if one fails to save life. More difficult to bear is the blame, often so unjustly laid to the charge of even the most careful and skilful physician.

Sometimes, indeed, a charge is made, if not with the intention of injuring him, at any rate as an excuse for leaving him and going to another. Patients are quite free to make such changes, though seldom wise, unless they are sure that the grounds for doing so are very good; but certainly care should be taken not to say anything not strictly true as an excuse for so doing.

But there are compensations—a doctor often become the patient's valued and trusted friend. And justly so, for though there are bad men in the profession they are, I am satisfied, fewer in proportion than in any other calling. The gratitude of patients, too, is often great and lasting. I am old, and years have elapsed since I had any under my care, but there be those who still remember me. This is manifested in many ways. But whether patients be grateful or not, it is a pleasure in the decline of life to know that this or that person has been restored to health, or their life saved though my instrumentality.

Looking back over that long space of time, it seems to me impossible for anyone to convey to the student of the present day an adequate idea of the revolution in the practice of medicine and surgery which has followed the great discoveries made in all branches of medical science within little more than half a century. Although insensibility had been produced previously by the inhalation of sulphuric ether, anaesthetics as we now understand them were unknown. Though water was known to swarm with animalcules, bacteria as a cause of disease was not dreamt of. Cholera and the allied diseases were looked upon as scourges to be combated as each man best could by the proper use of drugs, etc., but no one thought it possible to prevent the epidemic, when it occurred, from spreading except by the crude method of quarantine, or of tracing the cause of the original outbreak to its source. Patients suffering from all forms of fever, including small-pox, scarlatina, etc., were shut up in closely curtained rooms from which fresh air and light were excluded. Consumptives, in like manner, were kept indoors in close, warm, ill-ventilated rooms. Any old woman was deemed good enough for a nurse; and cleanliness, as regarded the utensils in the sick-room, little thought of. Bleeding, though going out, was still practised, and the application of leeches frequent. Perhaps, in this respect, the reaction against any form of blood-letting is being carried too far.

My recollections of the leading men of the profession at the time I joined it, and of the kindness I received from some of these, are amongst the pleasantest memories of my old age. Crampton, Marsh, Stokes, Corrigan and Graves were medical men second to none in their day, and had raised the reputation of the Dublin School of Medicine high in public esteem.

Sir Philip Crampton, though still on the staff of the Meath Hospital, was well-nigh past work, only coming occasionally to see an operation or as a consultant. He was a handsome old man with a fine presence, and was in the habit of driving himself about in a high mail phaeton, well horsed. In it he nearly ended my career during my first year, for, as I was leaving Trinity College one morning, he turned so suddenly out of Nassau Street into Grafton Street as I was in the act of crossing that I barely had time to save myself by throwing my hands against the near horse's chest; fortunately the horses, though high steppers, were not going fast and I got off with a shaking.

Graves and Carmichael were both still living. Of the former great physician I knew but little. He had ceased to be connected with the Meath before I was apprenticed; Carmichael met his death by drowning in a sad way; riding across the strand at Sutton to reach his country house, he was overtaken by the tide, which was running in strongly, and mistaking his course his horse stumbled; he was thrown into deep water and perished. He was a very charitable man, and to his donation of a large sum of money the success of the Medical Benevolent Society of Ireland is mainly due. He was a good surgeon, though not so well known as others I have mentioned.

Stokes I was fortunate to have as a teacher, and to count as a kind friend in after-life—a man of great ability, but of varying moods. At one time he would be a genial and delightful companion, full of anecdote, and then, again, he would be quite the reverse, remaining, even in genial company, quite silent. He has kept me for half an hour chatting in his study, though I told him his waiting-room was full of patients. He was indifferent, too, about making money, and died a comparatively poor man. He was a most reliable consultant, though occasionally he would give his opinion in a way that astonished the regular attendant. Thus, being called in to see an old lady, whose relatives had been told by the attending physician that her case was hopeless, he surprised the latter by saying, " I think that old lady will pull through." "Why," was the rejoinder, "has she not so and so?" entering fully into his views of the case. "Yes," replied Stokes, "you are quite right, but I know all about her; her life is no use to anybody, and I think she will recover." And I believe his prognosis proved true.

Very different was his contemporary, Sir Dominic Corrigan. Dr. Alfred Hudson—who for many years enjoyed a large practice, and was loved by all who knew him—called Stokes "the poetry" and Corrigan "the prose" of medicine —a most apt phrase.

Corrigan had for years the largest practice in Ireland. He wast very particular about his fees, and necessarily so, for a large number of the patients who thronged his waiting-rooms were members of the lower middle class from the country districts, who not infrequently tried to evade paying the fee. An amusing illustration of this came to my knowledge in this manner: —

I was elected registrar of the College of Physicians at the end of Sir Dominic's first year's tenure of office as president. It was a very busy time with me, for the building of the new college had just commenced, in which the president took an active interest, and he directed me to report to him every matter of any importance which might occur in reference thereto, or any college matter I might want advice about, so I not infrequently called at his house during his consultation hours. I used to wait in the hall till the patient came out of his study, when he always saw me at once, his manservant, who had been for some time in his service, used, while I waited, to entertain me with various scraps of semi-professional news. Calling one day, I found this man gone and a new man in his place, with whom I had a chat. About a fortnight elapsed ere I called again, and on doing so I said, "I hope you are getting on well." "Oh, no," he replied; "I am leaving to-morrow." Asking the cause, he told me this story: "It was a simple thing," he said; "there were a great lot of patients waiting to see the doctor the other day, and amongst them a lady from Cork. Well, the doctor had to go away before; he had seen them all; this lady was among those left and was greatly put out, saying she had come all the way just to see him. I said, 'Don't mind; come early to-morrow, and I will take care you see him at once.' Well, she gave me a shilling, and I put her in first the very next day. All went on well till she was leaving the study without giving the fee. So the doctor says,

'My fee, ma'am.' 'Your fee?' says she; 'did not I give the man in the hall a shilling?' He called me in and asked me was this true, and I said it was, and he gave me warning at the minute; but, you know, the place would not be worth holding if it was not for what the patients give. I burst out laughing, and, at that moment the study door opened, and Sir Dominic, hearing me laugh, asked what it was about. I told him, and he said it was quite true, and joined in the laugh himself.

No doubt it was usual for doctors' servants to look out for tips from patients, but for this woman coolly to pretend that she thought a shilling given to the servant constituted the doctor's fee is a good illustration of Irish character amongst a certain class, and their "'cuteness" in finding an excuse to try and evade paying the debt.

But such meanness is far from being universal. Personally I have no reason to complain of patients of the class of which I have spoken; they generally dealt fairly with me; indeed, the very opposite principle influences some—namely, that unless the doctor is paid an adequate fee he would not do his best for them. Thus, on one occasion, a woman of evidently quite the poor farmer class was ushered info my consulting-room. She came from a remote district in Connaught, wore neither bonnet nor hat, merely the customary shawl over her head. I soon detected that her case was hopeless; she suffered from a terrible complaint in such an advanced stage that I feared she might die ere she reached her distant home. So I advised her to return the next day, and that I would write to the local doctor, though she had not brought any introduction to me. She thanked me, asked me my fee, and paid it, asking, further, what the fee would be the next time she came. I said that as she had not, I presumed, much money to spare, I would not ask for any fee the next time, adding that I strongly advised her to return home at once. She withdrew, and another patient was ushered in, on whose departure my servant came in, and said that the country woman wished to speak to me again, when she said she thought me very kind, but that she wished to remain in town, and that she preferred paying the "regular thing "—that is, a guinea— every time she came to me. Suspicion is a very strong characteristic of all classes of the Irish peasantry.

Sir Dominic Corrigan died rather suddenly while still in active practice. The Fellows of the College of Physicians elected him president five times consecutively, an honour never previously conferred, and which he fully deserved, for it was through his instrumentality the present handsome college was erected, and to the end of his life he took the greatest interest in all college matters. To me he was the kindest of friends.

Sir Henry Marsh, though an older man, was a contemporary of Stokes. He had a very large and fashionable practice, was fond of show, kept a number of handsome horses, and for coachman the best whip in Ireland. He always dashed through the streets at a great pace, which, had it not been for the skill of his coachman, would have been dangerous. He was not genial like Stokes, and, probably from his somewhat distant manner, not popular amongst the rank and file of the profession, though liked by his personal friends, whom he sought chiefly amongst the aristocracy.

Dr. Thomas Beatty, who had a very large practice, was one of the most popular men of his day; he was alike a favourite with the members of his profession, with the public, and with his patients. He was a fine-looking man, with a ruddy, hairless face; had a beautiful though not strong voice, and sang sweetly; was full of amusing anecdotes, specially relating to medical, men of a previous generation, told to him by his father, who also had been a medical practitioner; in fact, he was a regular *raconteur* and in all respects a delightful after-dinner companion. I regret that I have now forgotten most of the stories I heard him relate, but the following I can give correctly:—

Mr. Solomon Richards, who died in 1819, was in his day a leading Irish surgeon. He had the reputation, of being the fattest and biggest-surgeon in the United Kingdom. Ireland at the beginning of the nineteenth century was in a most unsettled state—even the roads about Dublin were not safe after dark, robberies, and even murders not being uncommon.

Well, Richards was called on to perform an operation near Santry, a village some ten miles from Dublin, and was detained with the patient till long after sunset. It was winter, and he was returning in his carriage, having with him a Dr. Obré, who had called him in, a physician at that time in good practice, and who was as spare and insignificant as Richards was the reverse. Suddenly the carriage was stopped, and a footpad, opening the door on the side next which Richards sat, presented a pistol and demanded his purse. Richards, begging him to lower his pistol, handed him the purse, and then his watch, which the robber demanded. Then followed the demand, "Have you anything else?" "Yes," replied Richards; "here is my case of instruments," handing them out promptly. All this time Obré was concealed—hid by Richards's huge frame, which, in the dark, seemed to fill the carriage—and the footpad, not observing him, called to the coachman to drive on, but Richards stopped him, saying, "Oh, no; not till you speak to my friend on the other side of me." So Obré, too, thus pointed out, was relieved of his money and watch. Then the robber politely said "Good-night." But Richards was not yet done with him, and said, "My friend, you would not have got that gentlemen's money had it not been for me. now, my instruments won't bring you ten shillings on Charles Street" (a street which was, and still is, the mart for all kinds of second-hand tools and iron), "while to me they are of value. I think you might give me them back." "Well, I will," was the prompt reply, and the case was handed in. "One word more," said Richards; "you will get very little for that old watch. I care for it because it was my father's. Let me have it." "Well, you are a decent fellow," said the robber; "here it is." Then they drove on. Obré then, in great anger, broke the silence, and in unmeasured terms abused Richards, declaring that it was mean of him to point him out, as otherwise he would have escaped. Richards let him talk for a while, and then quietly said, "Do you think I was going to allow you to boast in the club tomorrow how well you got off while Richards was robbed? Oh, no; if I was to be robbed you must be also." Dr. Beatty assured me that this story was strictly true.

Beatty was not only good company, but enjoyed a good dinner thoroughly, and, to secure good care for himself at public dinners, made it a rule to tip the waiter beforehand liberally. He told me the following amusing incident in connection therewith:—

The dinner was at the Mansion House, where in old days hospitality was lavish. Everything was good and plentiful save that Beatty had some difficulty in getting as much bread as he wished for, and, having had to ask for a fresh supply of it more than once, apologised to the waiter, saying, "You see, I eat a deal of bread with my meat." "Yes, sir," replied the waiter, "and a deal of meat with the bread."

Everyone liked Beatty, and we all felt much regret that his declining years were saddened. First his wife died; then his only daughter, whom he idolised, made a match of which he did not approve. She and her husband, a doctor, lived in a remote part of Ireland, and he saw little, if anything, of her subsequently; while his only other child, a son, grievously disappointed him. To me he was the kindest of friends.

Dr. Montgomery, one of the professors in the University of Dublin, was an eloquent speaker, but a very different man from Beatty. He was small, but not insignificant-looking, and had a great idea of his personal appearance, of which he was vain. He always wore a white tie, and a diamond stud in his shirt front. It was told of him that he caused no little merriment at a dinner party— all the guests being medical men—where the conduct of a lady said to be fast was discussed, it being stated that her husband was very jealous of her. Montgomery took no part in the conversation for some time, but a pause occurring, said, "Well, gentlemen, I don't believe one word of those stories. Mrs ——has been my patient for months past. I have seen her over and over again alone in her house and at mine, and I can assure you Captain—— never once showed the least jealousy of me." At this time Montgomery was long past seventy, and looked it.

I have pleasant recollections of many others, who, though senior to me, were more or less my contemporaries—Dr. Samuel Gordon, Alfred Hudson, Sir William Wilde, Robert Mayne, and others. Gordon, the colleague of Sir Dominic Corrigan, and Dr. Alfred Hudson, were both charming men—genial, but quiet and unassuming in manner, esteemed by their professional brethren, loved by their patients. Sir William Wilde, the oculist, was brusque in manner and as wild in appearance as his name, a great conversationalist, and a welcome guest everywhere.

Gordon, though a retiring man, was full of quiet humour; he told a story well. One of himself amused us much. A country woman, a farmer's wife, consulted him, her main complaint being that she constantly "reefed up wind," meaning thereby frequent eructations, no doubt kept up by the habit so common amongst the lower orders, at least in Ireland, of forcing such. Dr. Gordon prescribed for this woman asafoetida pills. Some months elapsed before he saw the patient again; he had forgotten all about her, so he again prescribed the same pills. She took the prescription and looking at it said, "Why, this is the same old asafoetida pills again; they did me no good." Gordon hesitated a moment, and then asked her how she took them, and was told that she "swallowed them with a drop of water." "That, ma'am, was your mistake," he gravely said. "You should hold them in your mouth, chew them well, and swallow them slowly." She went away quite pleased to try the new method of taking pills.

I had the good fortune to know and enjoy the friendship of many of the leading men amongst the Fellows of Trinity College, Dublin, in my day. The Rev. John H. Jellett, who was provost, had been my tutor, and on his being appointed a professor, in 1848, I was transferred to Dr. Carson's care. He subsequently became vice-provost; and both were amongst my kindest as they were my most valued friends in after-life. I was also honoured by the friendship of the late provost, Dr. Salmon, who to his great abilities added a most genial manner, and was a delightful host. He was in the habit, as he left chapel on Sunday morning, of inviting some of the Fellows to breakfast with him, and, as I was frequently present, often included me amongst those invited. These friendly reunions were very pleasant. His death was a great loss to the college. He was a great man. His wife predeceased him by many years. On her tombstone is engraved this brief epitaph: —

"*The heart of her husband did safely trust in her.*"

These words truly express their mutual relations. Her death was a grievous affliction, but she left a daughter who to a great degree filled her place and was his true and faithful companion till his death.

Dr. Jellett was a very handsome man; he died while comparatively young. After the disestablishment of the Irish Church he took a very active part in the proceedings which ended in its successful reconstruction. He was a frequent speaker during the debates in the Synod on the revision of the Liturgy. He was a nervous man, and showed this when commencing to speak, which he always did with great lucidity. Rising generally at the conclusion of the debate, he not infrequently summed up the arguments of the previous speakers with great terseness and vigour. This led to the epigrammatic words spoken by Dr. Alexander, the venerable Primate of the Church of Ireland, on one of these occasions:

" He (Dr. Jellett) is the clarifier of the intellect of the country party," meaning thereby the representatives in the Synod, lay and clerical, coming from country districts, and this in consequence of the powerful influence his words had on them; and to the day of his death he was often spoken of as the "clarifier." He was a kind friend to me, and I greatly regretted his untimely death.

Dr. Carson was endowed with the possession of a wonderful memory. He knew the Bible virtually off by heart, and if you quoted a text, he could go on and repeat the whole chapter; and woe to you if you misquoted in his presence, you would be corrected instantly!

He was the terror of the unprepared undergraduate, and there were endless stories of his strictness. I much doubt if they were all well founded. In my own case he examined me for my "Little Go," which in the University of Dublin means the examination held at the end of the second university year. At that time I was a perfect stranger to him, and was greatly afraid lest I should fail, for in my position to fail would have been a very serious matter. Well, having translated a bit of a Latin author, he told me to read a passage he pointed out. I was ever but a poor classical scholar, but I knew that there was a "catch" somewhere in it—where, I did not know; so I read it in a remarkable manner, hoping by a guess to hit off the unknown snare. Having finished, he smiled, as was his invariable habit when he caught a man in the wrong, and said, "Mr. Atthill, most men make one mistake in that passage, but you have made two." With that he dismissed me, crestfallen and in terror; but I need not have feared, his opinion of my answering was not a very bad one.

Many years after, when I was the trusted medical attendant of his wife, whose life, if I could not save, I certainly prolonged, I reminded him of that incident—I rather think he was dining with me—and we laughed heartily at it.

CHAPTER XVI

RENEWING MY YOUTH

I take once more to yachting—My boatman's only compliment—The growth of my yachts—A 20-tonner—Yachting not an unmixed pleasure—An anxious night at sea—We shelter in Lough Ryan —Kept in Douglas Harbour during six days of storm—Men who are not yachtsmen.

T<small>O</small> MANY professional men who have lived an active life the retiring from practice is a great trial. They feel as did Sir Astley Cooper, who, having bought an estate in Yorkshire, sold his house in London, settling down, as he believed, to enjoy a happy old age in the country, only to find the want of actual employment unbearable. So he returned to town and resumed his practice. Others struggle on, clinging to their work, though mental and physical powers have deteriorated. Fortunately, it was not so with me, and feeling that I was less capable than formerly of doing my duty to my patients, I felt but little regret at giving up work, and since then time has never hung heavy on my hands.

Even before I had entirely withdrawn from practice I had taken up yachting once more, for I had never lost my taste for it. But now that I was able to enjoy this pleasant sport again, I was glad to find I retained something of my old skill in handling the sails and in steering. The boatman I took out with me had frequently expressed his scorn about the sailing of amateurs, but one day he asked me, "Is it long since you kept a yacht?"

"A good bit over forty years," I replied.

"Well," said he, "then you do not steer too badly."

That is the only compliment I ever received from him, but heard a great deal less about amateurs after it. Sailors do not care for the owner to take the sailing of a yacht into his own hands, if they can help it, and often try to make him feel that he knows nothing about it.

That little yacht soon gave place to a larger, and then to one of twenty tons, in which I used to spend many weeks at a time, going to Scotland and elsewhere almost every year, till old age, with its loss of ability to withstand the fatigue and exposure necessarily incidental to seafaring, compelled me very reluctantly to give up yachting altogether.

The pleasure I used to experience in sailing a well-found yacht on a fine day, with a fresh breeze blowing, was the greatest I have ever had. The pure air blowing in one's face; the bright sun; the glittering sea; the dash of spray that comes on deck or, it may be, sprinkles one's face as the boat throws the water off her bows; the feeling as you meet with the helm; of the vessel's incessant tendency to swerve from her course as the force of the wind or her sails lessens, increases, or varies in direction, and makes one almost fancy she must be a living thing—these, with the motion as the vessel dances over the waves, are all exhilarating to a degree; and the man who at such times retires into his cabin to pass the time in reading, smoking, or in sleep, does not deserve to he called a yachtsman; yet there are many such. But yachting is far from being an unmarred pleasure. The fine bright day may become wearisome from lack of wind. A flat calm (I speak of sailing yachts) is more trying than a gale of wind, for if in the latter there be anxiety and discomfort, the absolute helplessness, the result of a calm, tries one's patience. Then you may have first the one and then the other following closely. If after storm comes the calm, so after the calm may come the storm.

Thus on one occasion returning from the Clyde we sailed from Lamlash at 6 a.m.—for I wanted to get home—with a light breeze blowing in our favour. We carried all possible sail, setting even a large spinnaker, but even so we only made Ailsa Craig at 6 p.m., some thirty miles in twelve hours. I dined about then. I had no companion other than the two sailors, so was not long below; but, on coming up on deck, I found all changed. The sun was hidden by heavy clouds, it had become chilly, and the wind was rising; the glass, too, had commenced to fall. We took in sail at once, and then put down a reef in the mainsail, for the wind had become strong, and we had the night before us.By the time this was done it was eight o'clock; then, having lit our lamps, I told the men to go and lie down and that I would keep the first watch till midnight, when they would relieve me.

Soon it began to rain heavily, and, though I had on a suit of good oilskins and a sou'-wester, was wet through before twelve o'clock. But the wetting was the least part of the trouble. The darkness became inky—I could not see beyond the end of the bowsprit. Then I heard the noise of steamers all round me as they came down from Glasgow. We were right in their course! There the danger lay, for they might easily fail to see us as they came up from behind. We had no light aft, and I could not fail remembering that not many years previously a nephew of mine had been run down by one of these Glasgow steamers, in a small yacht at night, and that, though his sailors escaped, of him or his yacht no tidings were ever heard. I need not say I did not like the proximity of these steamers.

At about 11 p.m. I made out Corsewall Light, situated at the extreme south-west end of the Clyde. I only got a glimpse of it for a few minutes; then it was lost to sight in the inky darkness. The wind had changed and now nearly headed us. The tide too was running against us. A little before twelve, one of the sailors came on deck. I told him that I believed we might be a little way outside Corsewall Point, but that I had lost the light for some time.

Before taking the tiller the man went forward to look

if our light were burning well, and peered into the darkness that surrounded us; then after a minute or two exclaimed, "What light is that I see?" I, too, saw it. It was Corsewall, which a break in the clouds permitted me to see again. I had not realised how slowly we were sailing with a strong tide against us. As the wind was increasing, and as we had still some shelter from the land, I decided not to attempt to cross to Belfast, but to lie-to till daylight off the lighthouse. This we did. Soon after 3 a.m. we were able to see the outline of the coast, and as it was now blowing a whole gale, we took in another reef in our mainsail and sought safety in Lough Ryan, a sheltered but shallow bay, which lies behind Corsewall Point. It was six o'clock before we reached a safe anchorage. Wet and weary, I had been at the helm from 8 p.m. without any intermission. Then we all turned in and slept. Such is the open side of a yachtsman's life; but though I was not sorry to get back to the comforts of home, I was, in a day or two, quite ready to be off again.

Another time, after a delightful run, we anchored at night in Douglas Harbour, to find in the morning a gale of wind blowing and heavy rain falling. There we lay for six days, during the whole of which time the rain never ceased, and if we went ashore, it was clad in oilskins and wearing sea-boots. That also was not a pleasant experience. Nevertheless, did health and strength permit, I would be off yachting still.

My great difficulty always was to get a suitable companion for these cruises. Young men who like jollifications on shore, and perhaps a good deal of grog, did not care to come with me, or I prefer their company; and middle-aged men were too busy or did not like the sea. One friend sailed often with me. He was a first-class yachtsman and a nice fellow. Death, alas, deprived me of his society.

My experience is that comparatively few men who keep yachts really care for yachting. They like a sail of a fine day; they like the excitement of racing against vessels of their own class; they like, if well off, to entertain their friends on board; but they get sick of it if bad weather comes on, bringing with it discomfort, or the tedium of being weather-bound in some out-of-the-way harbour. Of course, the owners of steam yachts are not yachtsmen in the proper acceptation of the term, any more than the owners of a motor or motor-bicycle are whips or cyclists.

But though yachting is for me a thing of the past, and though I can now cycle but a very short distance, time, thank God, does not ever lie heavy on my hands. Each day brings its occupations.

CHAPTER XVII

FURTHER RETROSPECT

Advantages of the medical profession—An ungrateful patient—
Unappreciative patients—The question of fees—The Australian lady and
her generous husband— Success in cases, not money, the delight of doctors—
Undeserved credit—the too obedient patient—Some false teeth stories—Old
age something to be proud of—Going to extremes.

L OOKING BACK on my professional life, extending
as it does over quite half a century, and bearing in
mind all the anxieties, worries, and disappointments
incident thereto, I would nevertheless, had I to begin life
again, choose the profession of medicine in preference to
any other calling. For one thing, I have always felt that in
it a man is more independent and has greater freedom in
the use of his personal exertions than in any other; given
an opening, and nearly everything else depends on the
use he makes of it.

I hardly know which is now my predominant feeling
as I think of old times and of former patients—regret,
akin to pain, at the recollection of the ingratitude shown
by a few, or the pleasing memories of the gratitude,
kindly feeling, and friendship manifested by so many.
Human nature is prone to bear in mind the annoyances
of life, and to forget the pleasures and blessings.

The ingratitude of one patient I shall never forget. I was a young man when I attended her during a very serious illness, and as the nurse she had was one of the old school, and disposed to think more of her own comfort than of the patient's needs, I did various things the nurse should have done for her, and I ever believed that she owed her life to my unremitting attendance. She lived two miles from me, yet I visited her for a considerable time two or three times a day, for I could not trust the nurse, without seeking any remuneration for my extra visits. When convalescent she was profuse in her thanks, but not long after I heard that she said I should never again enter her house. Nor did I.

I recollect my old friend Mr. Collis telling me one of his experiences. He attended many patients gratuitously whom he knew to be poor, amongst these a widow lady, who was dying slowly of cancer and who, though unable to pay a fee, would send for him unnecessarily and at unreasonable hours. She had two daughters who earned a scanty livelihood as governesses. One of these daughters, after her mother's death, married a gentleman with good means, and got into society. From that day, she ignored Mr. Collis, and seemed to have forgotten his former kindness and liberality; but Sir Henry Marsh's carriage was to be seen frequently at her door, he being then the fashionable physician. Of this, of course, Mr. Collis took no notice; but one day a lady came to his house bearing a letter from his former patient, the ex-governess, saying that, knowing of old his great kindness to those who were poor, she sent this patient who was not able to give a fee, and trusted that he would prescribe for her. Mr. Collis proved that he deserved the title of "good," for he placed this lady on his long list of gratuitous patients.

My own experience, corresponds with that of Mr. Collis, namely, that patients from whom you do not take a fee not infrequently show but little gratitude—the thing which costs nothing seems but little valued. I say the same with even greater emphasis with respect to patients who, in consequence of their supposed inability to pay the usual fee, you treat with consideration. Many patients do not appreciate your kindness.

This was exemplified in a somewhat comic manner in the case of a young lady who came under my own care suffering from an ailment which, though causing discomfort and occasionally showing painful symptoms, did not interfere with her general health. She and her sister lived in apartments, and I had reason to believe that their means were somewhat limited; so being anxious to lessen the expense illness entails, I was careful to fix the dates on which she should again consult me as far apart as possible, as well as being considerate in the matter of fees. She continued under my care for about three months; then, being of opinion that treatment should be discontinued for a little time, and that change of air was desirable, I advised her to accept an invitation she had received to visit friends in the country. To this she agreed.

The date I had fixed for seeing her again had passed, when one afternoon I received a telegram from a medical man practising in Bray, some twelve miles from Dublin, requesting me to see a patient of his there with the least possible delay. I went as soon as possible, and to my surprise found that it was my own patient I was called to consult about. I had supposed her to be in the North of Ireland. It came out that, instead of adopting my advice, she had gone to a physician well known to be very particular about his fees, and had placed herself under his care; that she had seen him twice a week, and to be able to keep her appointments with him moved only this short distance from town. But being taken suddenly ill during the night she had sent for the local medical man, who, alarmed at her condition, telegraphed for this doctor under whose care she said she was. Finding that this doctor was from home, he wired to me, not knowing that the lady had been a patient of mine. I only saw her that one time. I know she recovered from that attack but of her future history I am ignorant. Of this I am sure, that medical attendance cost her three times as much as had she remained under my care. I believe, had I accepted regularly my usual fee from her, I Should have retained my patient.

Some patients are fond of changing their medical

attendant. They are quite free, but seldom wise to do so, and had better not, without good reason. On one occasion a lady consulted me, telling me she had been a patient of my friend Dr. Kidd, but had left him to come to me. Finding that she lived in a remote part of Ireland, I asked her if she knew Mrs. ———, who resided in that district. She said "that they did not visit, but that she had seen her in Dr. Kidd's waiting-room a few days before." So his patient came to me, and mine went to him at just the same time. I never cared for this class of patients.

The question of fees is sometimes troublesome. For my own part I had little to complain of in this respect. As a physician I kept no books, and as a rule received my fee then and there. Sometimes a patient would ask, "Will you allow the fees to lie over for the present?" and I invariably said "Yes," not always wisely. Thus on one occasion a lady, the wife of a captain in the Line, made this request. She was under my care for some time, and got much better, so I said she need not come to me any more. She asked me how much she was in my debt. I knew her husband to be a member of a good but far from wealthy family, and she had, moreover, more than once spoken of their means being limited; so I said, "Ten guineas, but as you tell me your means are limited, if your husband sends me five it will do." She thanked me warmly for my liberality and said that a cheque would be sent that night; but it did not come, and a few days later

I saw in the paper that the couple had sailed for India, I never heard from them. Comment needless.

But there is a reverse side. Some months after the foregoing incident occurred, an Australian lady came under my care. She was in very delicate health and she told me her husband would come for her when she was fit to return. She continued under my care for a good while, and when her husband arrived he was greatly pleased at finding her health so much improved. A day was fixed for their departure, and still nothing was said about paying me for my attendance, and it was not till I was actually saying good-bye, on the day before they were to start, that her husband said,—

"By the way, I am in your debt; how much is it?"

I replied that I really hardly knew; that I kept no books, but that it could not be less than five-and-twenty guineas.

"Twenty-five guineas!" he repeated after me. "You would not do for the colonies. Well, I will fill up the cheque for fifty, anyway," and so he did. Nor was it more than fair remuneration, but I could never bear that it should be said I tried to get as much as I could from a patient, and in such a case as this always named a lesser sum than I was entitled to. I was, however, particular in naming a sufficient fee when asked to go long distances to the country, because leaving town is a serious matter for a man who sees numerous patients during his consulting hours; his absence disappoints them and injures himself.

But the amount of money received is not, with the great majority of medical men, that which gives them a pleasure at all equivalent to the gratification they feel at the satisfactory termination of a serious illness, and the knowledge that they have been the instruments of saving life, or at least restoring to health, some who might otherwise have remained sufferers. The ingratitude of a patient cannot destroy that!

One cannot help smiling, even after the lapse of many years, when one remembers how one gained credit when little was due, and contrasts this with the occasions when one gained little or none when much was deserved. A patient often fancies that some trifling symptom is of great importance, and if relieved by simple means magnifies the "cure." Thus, when I was just beginning to get some consulting practice, a medical friend sent a lady to me who fancied she needed the advice of a specialist. Before describing her symptoms she informed me that she had been under the care of Sir James Simpson, of Edinburgh, and that she had consulted other eminent medical men without deriving benefit. Having examined her carefully I came to the conclusion that she had no real disease, but that probably she lived too well and took too little exercise, and prescribed for her a simple medicine consisting mainly of a bitter infusion, containing a good proportion of Epsom salts. I thought no more about her, but after the lapse of a few weeks I received a letter from the doctor who had sent her, asking me to read a letter he enclosed. This was from the lady he had recommended to me. In it she wrote to this effect: "You know I have been with Sir James Simpson, and with So-and-so in Paris and Berlin, but none of them have done me any good except Dr. Atthill!"

No medical man can be successful who fails to gain the confidence of his patients, and no patient can be satisfactory who does not trust him. But even confidence can be carried so far as to produce unexpected and inconvenient results as happened to myself more than once—markedly so in one case.

I had arranged to take my annual holiday when, on the day preceding that on which I was to start, I was asked to see a patient on whom I found that a serious operation must be performed at once. So I postponed my departure and operated without delay. She made such an excellent recovery that at the end of a week I went off, leaving her under the care of the gentleman who had brought her to me, telling him that she did not need any special treatment, and that he could allow her to sit up soon.

I was absent for nearly a month, and on my return Went at once to inquire for her. To my surprise I found her in bed. I asked her, had she been out to drive? "No."

Had she walked out? "No." So by degrees I learned that she had not even sat up in the bed yet; and at last discovered that as I had after the operation told her she must lie on her back for a time, and had forgotten to say to her before starting that she might change her posture, she had refused to do so till I gave her leave; so on her back she lay for the whole time I was away. She was one of those grateful patients. She went home and I never saw her again, but for many years every Christmas brought me a pretty card painted by herself, the receipt of which always gave me much pleasure.

As a rule the sick-room is not a place to cause a smile, still it can hardly be avoided sometimes. I had as a patient a nice old lady. I never heard her exact age, but her younger sister who lived with her told me she herself was seventy-five.

One day calling to see her—she had become virtually bedridden—she complained of her mouth being sore, and as she made difficulties about my looking at it, I asked, had she any false teeth? To which she replied quite tartly, "There is nothing artificial about me!" As I left the house her companion, an elderly lady who had lived with her for thirty-five years, went downstairs with me. To her I said,—

"Is it possible that those nice white teeth Mrs. —— has are her own?"

"I do not know," was the reply, "but every now and

then she will send me out of the room, saying she wants her sister to do something for her, and I think it must be to have her teeth taken out and cleaned."

A few days later the old lady told me she had "some false teeth." On the day when I asked about the teeth, I saw in consultation another very old lady who was dying of cancer. Her daughter had told me that her mother was long past eighty; that she was very exacting and difficult to please; in fact she was one of those querulous old women who render the life of those about them almost intolerable. Having examined her, she addressed me to this effect: "I hope you will be able to do something for me. I do not like to think of those young things being left without someone to care for them (her youngest daughter had told me that she was forty-eight). I am getting old; I suppose I must be nearly seventy."

It is strange that old people on the verge of the grave should try to conceal the fact that they have false teeth. Or to deceive as to their age, yet this is common, and by no means confined to the female sex. I rather feel that old age is something to be proud of. One thing I have dreaded since old age has overtaken me, that is, that I should become a helpless, useless invalid, perhaps as querulous and as exacting as some of those I have known—say, as an old lady I knew of, who would not allow the window shutters to be opened in the room in which she lay bedridden for many months, and yet compelled a grandchild to sit nearly the whole day in the dark, grumbling if, when she went for a walk, she was not back, in half an hour, No wonder I fear lest I should become one of such! and, alas! they are many. To me sudden death has always seemed the most merciful termination of life, and I could never join in that sentence of the Litany in which we are asked to pray "from sudden death. Good Lord, deliver us," though, of course, to the relations and friends the sudden death of a loved one is a terrible shock.

When I was young, every sick person was bled from the arm or covered with leeches; every bed was surrounded with curtains which were drawn round it at night, and kept particularly close in the case of illness. The night air was commonly supposed to be unwholesome and laden with noxious miasma. As a young practitioner I must have held ideas somewhat in advance of my day, for I recollect trying to persuade an old lady I was attending that at least in a city the air at night must be purer than by day, because then there would be less in it, but I could not induce her to allow a window in the house to remain open at night. One wonders how so many patients in bygone days recovered, and why consumption is so vastly more prevalent now than then!

No one can be a greater advocate for pure air than I am, but I cannot shut my eyes to the fact that the admission of it into rooms is often so unwisely arranged that serious and, indeed, fatal illness follows from exposure to draughts of cold air from Open windows—this specially in the case of persons enfeebled by illness or old age. The human body will bear with impunity much cold if the individual be in fairly good health, and without shelter, even in inclement weather, will remain well; but many of these same people will contract attacks of a serious nature, when housed, from exposure to draughts from windows and open doors; and many lives are lost nowadays in consequence of ill-regulated ventilation. The human mind seems unable to avoid running into extremes.

CHAPTER XVIII

LAST RECOLLECTIONS

A new generation of doctors—Little changes, but examples of a great revolution—Changes at home and abroad—State of the country districts of Ireland—Guidance of affairs not in our hands—Deathbed scenes—I never thought death would be like this—An indelible impression—An answer to prayer—I did my best.

I HAVE OUTLIVED all my professional con-temporaries—at least, all of whom I have any knowledge. A new generation of physicians and surgeons occupy the places we once filled. Not a few of these were pupils of mine in bygone days; better men, too, without doubt, than their predecessors. Their education has been vastly superior to that we received, and their successes deservedly greater. But the progress of medical science is not yet stayed; they too, like us, must be content to be learners, or they will fall behindhand in the race. So, too, it is with other professions.

These truisms are obvious to every one, but are there not some of us in a great degree blind to the fact that, after all, these changes which we notice in our own little spheres are but examples of the great revolution going on with rapid strides over the whole world? The vast change in the social condition of the European nations can hardly have escaped the notice of the most careless. The North America of my childhood consisted of the "United States," occupying only that part of the continent east of the Mississippi, of two provinces named Upper and Lower Canada just struggling for existence, and a half-savage State called Mexico of which almost nothing was known. Africa was an unknown country, save only that "the Cape" was a place ships called at for their four or five months' voyages to or from India. Egypt, under the sway of the Porte, was a *terra incognita* beyond Alexandria, though a stray European might occasionally reach Cairo. Australia was only spoken of as a place convicts were sent to. As to New Zealand, I never heard it named. What Canada, Australia, and New Zealand are how every child knows.

But how many of us realise the revolution which has taken place in our own country within the recollection of those still living. Agricultural England, the source of pride, as well as the backbone of the nation during the wars arising out of the French Revolution, has fallen not alone from its high estate, but as a source of national wealth agriculture has ceased to exist. The population which lived on the land has migrated to the towns and now works in factories. The old country families are steadily, if gradually, disappearing, to be replaced to some extent by those fortunate enough to accumulate wealth as manufacturers or traders. The yeoman has disappeared, and cannot be replaced.

In Ireland the revolution is even more marked. As a result of the Land Acts, the landed gentry are vanishing rapidly; in another generation none will exist. Whether this total extinction will be an unmixed good remains to be proved. That many of that class were in the past improvident, careless and wanting in the qualities which would make them useful in their sphere is certain; a few were harsh towards their tenants, and some were unjust; but the vast majority, on the other hand, were kind, generous landlords, anxious for the welfare of those under them, and spending their incomes at home. The loss of such must be an injury to the community.

This change in the state of the country districts of Ireland has brought about a serious alteration in the class of medical men whose duty it is to take charge of the sick poor. Formerly, the selection of a doctor for a dispensary district lay in a great degree in the hands of the resident gentry, and they, as I can testify, exercised great care in the selection of the candidate to fill the vacant post. Now it has passed into the hands of the Poor Law Guardians, men unfortunately often incapable, from defective education, of choosing wisely, or who are wholly influenced in favour of someone brought forward by a local politician who cares for nothing except the promotion of his influence. The result is that unfit men are very liable to be elected, with disastrous results to the poor, who are helpless.

Further, if I read not the signs of the times wrongly,

tolerance will not exist in Ireland, either as respects religion or politics. I look with much apprehension on the future, though I shall not live to see it. But the guidance of the affairs of the nation is not in our hands any more than the regulation of times and seasons. Believing as I do that my path through life has been made plain to me, and my every step directed, I in like manner believe that the destinies of our nation will be guided by the all-wise providence of the Almighty.

I had, of course, my share of the sad and pathetic cases, which cannot fail to distress the physician, who often knows what is hidden from even near relatives, and whose duty it is to reveal nothing of what he sees or of what comes to his knowledge. The bodily health may be restored, but a broken heart cannot be healed, nor a career, commenced with well-grounded hopes of success but blighted by folly or sin, be re-established on its former footing. But in each and every case death too often closes the scene.

The doctor is but seldom present when the soul departs to the Lord who gave it. When that event is evidently in hand he can do no good and his presence is seldom desired. Of so-called deathbed repentance I have known no instance. Of those who died of chronic diseases, especially consumptives, the great majority are hopeful to an extraordinary degree, and death often comes to them suddenly and unexpectedly; and when acute cases end fatally, the mental faculties in the vast majority of instances are obscured some time before death comes—in my opinion, the act of a merciful God.

I have ever believed that as the tree falls, so does it lie—that be it man or woman, when the soul departs, it goes to the place they have prepared for themselves. The heaven the Christian believes in would be no place of happiness to the drunkard, the gambler, the dishonest, or the adulterer.

But I have stood by the deathbed of those for whom death had no terror. That of my old master, Mr. Collis, was a supremely happy one. He died of suffocative bronchitis, a most distressing affection. I called to inquire for him the afternoon of his last day on earth, and hearing I was in the house, he expressed a wish to see me.

On entering his room he beckoned me to his bedside. He was propped up, and breathing with great difficulty. So great was his distress that great beads of perspiration covered his forehead. On coming close he said to me, speaking with difficulty, "I sent for you because I wish you to see how a Christian can die." I thought then, and I pray now, that my end may be as his was, full of hope and joy.

Some years later I stood by another deathbed, that of a very different man. He was an old friend, and had been very kind to me. He was paralysed, and could only walk a few steps. His life had been a varied one. First, a clerk in his father's office, who was a London merchant. That position, he detested, and he longed to be a soldier. He adored his mother, but had no love for his father, who was a martinet and, he used to declare to me, jealous of him because of his mother's partiality. This was the time of the Peninsular War, and he told me he used always to sleep on the floor to inure himself to the hardship and discomfort incident to a soldier's life.

At last his father yielded to his importunity, and he was gazetted as an ensign in the 52nd Regiment, and as a lieutenant was present with that regiment at Waterloo. After the peace he was put on half pay, and remained on it till the day of his death. At first he hoped that he would be gazetted to some regiment, but time passing on without this being done, he went to Spain as representative of his father's house, and lived there for many years a gay and, I fear, a somewhat dissipated life. He did not marry till he was quite an old man, and his religious opinions were of the vaguest description. Being a kind-hearted and, indeed, generous man, he gave freely to the needy, but only to those whom he believed to be worthy of it.

On one occasion we had a rather lengthened conversation on religious matters, and I well remember his saying, in reply to some observation of mine, "Well, God is good and merciful, and I believe that on the Judgment Day He will say of me, 'Well,——has done a great deal

that is wrong, but he helped So-and-so in their troubles.'"
That, as I could understand it, was his hope for the
hereafter. He often spoke of death, and that he did not
fear it, and was ready to meet it whenever it came. Above
all, he regretted that he did not meet a hero's death in the
battlefield. Well, he met with a trivial accident, which, in
his unhealthy state, produced blood-poisoning. I sat by
his bedside after sunset the night before he died. He gave
me some directions about his funeral and his affairs, and
then dozed off. He slept quietly for half an hour, then
roused, turned in his bed, and in an undertone, as if
speaking to himself, said, "Death! is this death? I never
thought it would be like this." I was startled; he spoke
with such solemnity and, to me it seemed, with dread.

Those were his last articulate words; he became
comatose, and died the next day. His death was
painless—yet how different from the joy felt by my old
master, though the latter's sufferings were extreme!

I could not, were I inclined to do so, enumerate the
many occasions on which I felt sure that the Lord my
God cared for me and answered my prayer, sinful man
though I be. One occasion, more than forty years ago, is
indelibly impressed on my memory. I had been greatly
depressed, partly in consequence of the illness of a loved
member of my family, and from the fact that for some
time I had very little to do and, as it seemed, had ceased
to earn an income that would enable me to meet our

daily wants. Sunday came round, and as I sat waiting for the morning service to commence, I opened my prayer book at the 37th Psalm, verse 5, in which occur the well-known words, "Commit thy way unto the Lord; and put thy trust in Him; and He shall bring it to pass."

I felt at the time as if this was specially addressed to me and felt quite cheered. The confirmation of my belief that the message was sent to me came speedily.

On reaching my house after service I found a medical man waiting for me for the purpose of getting me to see a patient of his who was very ill. He further told me he wished to transfer the patient to me. Of course I gladly consented, and on our way to the patient's house he told me more about her. She was, I found afterwards, a very beautiful young woman, the wife of an officer, but possessed of a very violent temper, and a most difficult patient to manage. On the previous day her husband had hinted that he would have to leave home, and on this she had become so excited that he dare not mention the subject again, so had decided, after I had seen her with him, to go away without saying anything. She would not know until the following morning of his departure, when I was to call.

I found the patient very ill indeed, but our visit passed off very satisfactorily. As she lived some distance off in the country, I started to see her early the next morning, to be told on my arrival by the servant that her mistress would not see me, and that she had sent a groom some time before with a letter telling me not to come. I told the maid to say to her mistress that I had not received the letter, and that as I had come so far I hoped she would see me. I had to wait some time before I received an answer, but was at length shown up.

The patient received me most ungraciously, but her invectives were directed chiefly against her previous doctor, whose conduct she denounced in unmeasured terms.

After a little time I got in a word, but at first she refused to answer a question or give me any information as to her state; then, on my saying I was sorry that she would not allow me to try to relieve her, she suddenly burst into tears, saying that she was in such great pain she could hardly bear it. Finally she allowed me to examine her, and on doing so I felt no doubt as to the truth of her statement, and in a few minutes we were friends. I then told her that the application of a few leeches would not only relieve the pain, but also materially accelerate her recovery; she agreed that they should be applied, but only on the condition that this was done by myself. Neither nurse nor chemist would she allow to do it, so it was settled that her carriage should be sent for me in the evening. The leeches gave her great relief, and the next morning I had the satisfaction of finding a marked improvement in her condition. From that time on she was a most obedient patient, though her convalescence was tedious and trying.

I did not attain professional success from the possession of any special talents, save industry, if that be called such, and that, indeed, seemed to me to have been acquired. In my case, as I believe it is with others, an opening was made for me; my way pointed out, I did my best in the position assigned to me, always trying to learn. The man who believes in his own attainments rarely succeeds.

My axiom has always been, "Whatsoever thy hand findeth to do, do it with all thy might." That, and the verse already quoted, "Commit thy way unto the Lord; and put thy trust in Him; and He shall bring it to pass," containing a precept and a promise, I would earnestly commend to every one who may chance to read these, most probably the last, words of an old man who has seen much of the cares and trials incidental to all ranks and to all degrees, in this brief life on earth, where grief and sorrow are ever present.